ALL DRESSED UP AND NOWHERE TO GO

Malcolm Bradbury has pursued the careers of academic and writer with equal enthusiasm. Born in Sheffield, since 1970 he has been Professor of American Studies at the University of East Anglia at Norwich, and in addition lectures at universities both here and abroad.

He is also one of the sharpest and most penetrating social satirists writing in Britain today. Critically acclaimed and devotedly read, his bestselling novels include EATING PEOPLE IS WRONG, STEPPING WEST-WARD, WHO DO YOU THINK YOU ARE? (a collection of short stories) and THE HISTORY MAN, all of which are available in Arrow. THE HISTORY MAN was, of course, dramatized in a highly successful BBC television series in 1981.

He is a regular contributor to *Punch* and the *Tatler*, to television and radio programmes, and writes reviews for the national press as often as time allows.

ALSO IN ARENA BY MALCOLM BRADBURY

The History Man
The After Dinner Game
Stepping Westward
Eating People is Wrong
Who Do You Think You Are?
Rates of Exchange

Malcolm Bradbury

ALL DRESSED UP AND NOWHERE TO GO

An Arena Book
Published by Arrow Books Limited
62-65 Chandos Place, London WC2N 4NW

An imprint of Century Hutchinson Limited

London Melbourne Sydney Auckland
Johannesburg and agencies throughout
the world

First published in this revised edition by Pavilion Books
in association with Michael Joseph 1982
Arrow edition 1983
Arena edition 1986

Printed and bound in Great Britain by
Anchor Brendon Limited, Tiptree, Essex

ISBN 0 09 931890 3

TO
MICHAEL ORSLER

INTRODUCTION

I

One day at the end of the 1950s, long before monetarism, *Dallas*, and Legionnaire's disease, when the world was still quite young, two pelicans were seated on a warm current at the mouth of the Saint John's River, in Northern Florida, snapping their beaks at fish and eyeing each other quizzically, when they were interrupted by an unexpected sight. A battered, salt-caked freighter, no bigger than a large bedroom slipper, had penetrated through the well-nigh impassable shoals at the river's mouth, and was proceeding on an uncertain course up the estuary. A string of flags fluttered from the mastheads, proclaiming either that the pilot was on board, or the cholera was. But what attracted especial attention was the dull, ravaged figure, his features pasty-white, his clothes scuffed and battered, his eyes fixed on the foggy horizon with the myopic gaze of the true visionary, who stood at the ship's rail. His Rex Harrison hat and the thick tweed suit in which he sweated proclaimed him to be unmistakeably British. His socks somehow failed to match; something resembling a postgraduate thesis appeared to be tucked under one of his two armpits. 'Hullo, another goddam Columbus,' said the more observant of the pelicans; and they took off south to fulfil an old wing-flapping engagement they were booked for at the Fontainebleu in Miami.

Meanwhile the freighter staggered on on its disorderly course up the channel; the raddled figure by the rail staggered with it, desperately looking for harbour. It seemed to him extraordinary that only a mere six weeks before this he had been back at home in 1950's Britain, boarding, somewhere off a back street in Salford, Manchester, this same vessel, the M.S. *Necrophilia* – a fine sight then as she lay, her spars agleam, her brasswork shining, her crew gaily dancing hornpipes, at rest on the muddy bottom of the Manchester Ship Canal. It seemed to him even more extraordinary that he had started on his voyage a debonair and promising youth, a young Nottingham intellectual with five published articles to his credit, all in journals of absolutely no importance. A Nottingham intellectual may not seem on the face of it a demanding pastime; it is therefore worth remembering that in the later 1950s there was just as much angst, despair and hard thinking, and of just as good a quality, in Nottingham as there was anywhere else. For in those days the provinces were in; Nottingham was full of Jewish refugees called Grizelda, who played the harp in black stockings; in its espresso bars, under the heavy tropical greenery, lulled by the aphrodisiacal pulsing of Spanish guitars, the coffee-machines worked without steam, and the bright young writers and intellectuals steamed without work. For only shortly before this, John Osborne's play *Look Back in Anger* had tempted into existence a large motley crew of intellectual vagabonds and misfits who, when they were not sleeping in sleeping bags on Hampstead Heath, sat around in Nottingham and Leicester, drinking cups of broth and condemning the world, consumerism, Harold Macmillan, and virginity. And they dreamed dreams, above all of the United States, the land of modernity, freedom, space, jazz, spontaneity and, with luck, even a little sex as well.

Such, then, was the spirit of the quest that had driven this now broken figure on board the *Necrophilia*, determined to take the freighter route to America and the free and open life. Six weeks before, the fabulous voyage had begun, out past ancient Altrincham; it was only when three days had gone by, and the vessel, seemingly growing smaller by the hour, had still not made open sea, that the uneasy thought had begun to arise in our traveller's mind that perhaps not every omen surrounding his New World voyage was propitious. A mere ten days out, and Dublin was sighted. Here several more days were devoted to commerce, largely on the part of the mate, whose business it was to sell perfectly new hawsers to strange red-nosed men in unmarked vans; then the voyage proper commenced. Nosing round the southern tip of Ireland into the December gales, which had waited until February to find a ship as ill-equipped as this, the vessel began its Atlantic passage. Battered by storms, it responded magnificently, converting itself into a kind of submarine and advancing forward just a few feet below sea-level. Water came down the funnel frequently; the cargo, of ill-packed crates of Scotch whisky, now began shifting, needing the frequent attention of the crew; the captain, judging the weather, ordered that not only should the ship's furniture be screwed down, but the six passengers as well. Yet a mere six weeks later, the famous landfall had come, just that morning. The shouts of sailors sounded on deck, warning that the ship was about to run into a large hut marked Mcdonald's Hamburger; the captain was raised from his drunken stupor; maps were, with difficulty, found, and it was discovered that all this was consistent with having reached America.

It is hard, in these cynical times, to evoke that classic sense of wonder that has always occurred, throughout history, as the New World reveals itself in its marvellous novelty. But we may be sure our immigrant experienced it as, by a mere three in the morning, the gangplank was secured, and he descended at last into the new land, felt Florida underfoot, halted on the dockside, and shook his fist at the captain of the *Necrophilia* in a last malicious gesture of farewell. Then he turned to confront America: the land of the free, the home of the brave, the world of the modern and the new. There was a bare dock wall; two or three longshoremen stood in the shadow of the wharf, pilfering beef and arguing whether it was better to be written up by Eugene O'Neill or Arthur Miller. No form of transport was to be seen; the lights of the town shone, ridiculously far away, beyond a nexus of railroad tracks and waterlogged ditches in which alligators snapped at rusting Coke cans. A frost scarce in these parts seeped up the leg of the visitor's trousers. Wiping a tear of chagrin from his eye, and shouldering a metal footlocker that seemed to him neither smaller nor less weighty than the Empire State Building, in fabulous New York City, which he took to be just up the road, the figure lit out, sagging at the knees, into the territory that Christopher Columbus had once, in a not dissimilar state of confusion, discovered.

Yet, despite his bleak, late-night landfall, the stranger's arrival had not gone unnoticed. Indeed, throughout the Land of Liberty, preparations were at that moment being made for his arrival. In the immigration shed along the dock, officials were doing revision seminars in aggression and hostility. In great cities the length of his likely route, taxi-drivers were resetting the meters in their cabs; in hotels and motels clear across the nation, box-spring vibration-mechanism body-contoured mattresses were being removed from beds, and replaced with straw-filled sacks. In major research libraries everywhere, rare books were being removed from shelves and concealed in private homes, in case he wished to consult them. Thus, as he dragged his footlocker through the swamplands to the nearest Greyhound station, where the sailors slept on benches with their mouths open, and cleaners came round to brush his shoes with brooms as the daylight rose, America expected him, just as much as he expected America. Three hours later, on a dark-windowed bus going northwards, with the Spanish moss dripping over the long straight highway, the lavatory flushing just behind him, and a magazine on his knee displaying pictures of sunbathing beauties by a luxury pool, under the legend 'This Time, Try It By Freighter', the traveller began to reflect on his experience. It came to him then that not all was lost. There was probably a book in it, several books. For it is with literature as with diarrhoea;

nothing stimulates either as much as travel and cultural comparison.

II

It is as well to admit at this point that this gawping pioneer was, give or take a total lie or two, no other a person than my own early self, come to look for a new life somewhere beyond cosy, comfortable, confining 1950s Britain. I was not an angry young man, perhaps, since to me the angry young men were all old, ten years or so older than I was. But I was a niggling one, an uneasy figure struggling in my Englishness, fighting to get out. The British provinces had been swallowing me like an eiderdown; America seemed the great good place. I took the bus to New York, and rode in the endless elevator up to the top of the Empire State Building; below was the great metropolis, looking like a gigantic waffle-iron. Excitement grew; I took the ferry and sailed out to the Statue of Liberty, while fireboats sprayed me with jets of water; I wandered Macy's, and bought nylon shirts, then a new invention that made you ping with static electricity when you put them on and off. The Beat Generation was riding high: I went to poetry readings in gloomy bagel shops in Greenwich Village, where poets in dark glasses would look up at the ceiling and cry 'Come, little bird of poetry, fly down to me' (actually it rarely did). I talked to deviants on benches outside the New York Public Library, while dapper secretaries went by, carrying plastic Lord and Taylor's bags. It was different, exciting; yet I still didn't feel I knew what America was. Then one day the revelation came. I was staying with the parents of a Jewish friend in their small apartment in the Bronx. It was not a notable apartment, but it did have a notable American kitchen: a shining bulbous icebox, a glinting split-level cooker, Formica worktops, a whirring blender and mixer, a toaster that threw bread into the air as if in sport, and, in the middle of the sink, an object called a Dispose-All which consumed the kitchen refuse and sent it all straight to the sewage company. Commonplace now, it was a wonder of the fifties; I used to wander in there frequently, just to experience it all. One day my host came and found me there, staring down the Dispose-All's magnificent orifice, as if seeking the meaning of life. Not speaking, he opened the door of the icebox, took out an entire uncooked chicken, thrust the creature into the grinder, and switched on. Standing there, watching the machine consume the entire bird, I knew at last that I had seen the New World, and it worked.

I stayed on in the States for a long time, in the American heartland, teaching Freshman Composition – better known as Readin', Writin', Speakin' and List'nin' – at a university in a cornfield in the Middle West. Here I taught coeds in tight sweaters, cantilevered bras and Elizabeth Arden make-up, and seven-foot-tall footballers with crew cuts and huge ears, who could sit in the third row and still put their feet up on my desk ('Duh, I didn't doe dey was mine,' said one of them when, after five weeks, I complained). I taught them the simple things of life: how to use human language, how to write on pieces of paper from left to right, how to open books without splitting the spine, how to put in verbs to give a sentence the completeness of a sentence. I taught a lot, but I learned more. My students called for me in cars and took me out on dates, teaching me how to drink milkshakes; they showed me the way to the Doosie Duds, where I washed my socks, and the Piggly Wiggly, where I bought comestibles and acquired free Melamine tableware on food orders of five dollars or more. I thought I was growing American, though the students never quite agreed. 'Pip-pip, old chap,' they said as they came into class, 'Bin shootin? How's the Queen?' Indeed, as time went by, a certain excess of Englishness crept into my character. Though by origin a good deal closer to Jimmy Porter than the Duke of Windsor, I acquired a degree of bearing. My old cheap Harris tweed sports jacket with plastic patches on the elbow (only Oxbridge undergraduates could afford leather) acquired a fine old glow, as if it had been carefully smoked over a peat fire by willing peasants, and then systematically stained with claret by family butlers. I became an expert in politeness, rank, the Royal Family, hunting, and warm beer.

At the same time my literary ambitions were proceeding apace. For in addition to haunting the coffee bars of Nottingham, shouting about Sartre and nibbling the ears of leggy girls named Ernestine, I had spent three years being a student at a certain nameless English provincial university. A strange youth, who wore pink intellectual shirts and clip-on bow ties that kept falling off suddenly into cups of black coffee, I had spent most of those three years writing a novel, about, of course, an English provincial university. I used to sit for hours in the university entrance hall, ostentatiously correcting a large sheet of proofs: 'He's a writer,' my two or three friends would explain to any passing visitor who happened to stumble in, usually under the impression that they had found the public library. I had once seen T. S. Eliot, or someone very like him, emerge from the offices of Faber and Faber in Russell Square, so I felt alert to everything that was happening in the literary scene; I had even been discovered — by a college friend, the editor of the literary magazine, a man named Michael Orsler, an impressive figure who used to stand naked at the window of his room, shouting 'Sex rules the world' to occasional passing suburban shoppers. Everyone assured me that a book about an English provincial university would never sell, and this confirmed me in my integrity. It was to these talents that I now turned in my office in the midwestern heartland; passing strangers, wandering close to the English Department late at night, would hear the tapping of typewriter keys as I wrote down for posterity the benefits of my Anglo-American experience in articles that went to *Vogue* and *Harper's* and *Punch* and somehow managed to appear in print.

It all came to an end, of course. My contract ceased after a year. I posted the final grades on the door of my office and locked myself in, while disappointed students shouted through the keyhole in fury. I said goodbye to my friends, who explained that they had not understood a word I had said all year, because of my foreign accent. I knew, with a kind of dread in my heart, that it was time to go home to England. I knew that going home was always an agony, if not a disaster; that I would miss what I had enjoyed. I had learned much about America, in the Doosie Duds and the Piggly Wiggly and the long car and bus journeys I had taken right across the nation, there to find more Doosie Duds, more Piggly Wigglies, more and more and more. In a dark, or at any rate decidedly ill-lit, night of the soul, I put all my Melamine tableware into my great footlocker, heaved it lightly over one shoulder, and set off to walk the thousand or so miles to New York City and the Cunard Pier, on that most ancient of quests, the tale of return. Great liners with big red funnels still ran in those days, though plane-travel was becoming fashionable in some quarters. Looking forward to six days of leisure, I climbed aboard the grand vessel, a haven of Englishness, smelling of marchionesses, carbolic soap, and good old kippers. The freighter I had come on, all those lifetimes ago, would have made one of its lifeboats; 'Directions for Adjustment', said the notices on the wall of the underwater tourist cabin in which I found myself, showing a picture of a very well-developed girl strapping herself into some apparatus that made her look even more well-developed still. And adjustment, after a long spell of America, was exactly what I needed. For I looked around at my fellow-passengers, and the severe guardians who formed the crew. They appeared to me odd, until I realized that they were simply English. I would need to learn England all over again.

For five days I drank my bouillon and played deck-quoits with the best, convalescing from America. Then we suddenly emerged from the spray just off the Scilly Isles, and the old land was nearby, somewhere in the mist and the rain. The BBC News came over the loudspeakers, and the old high-toned voice of the British newscaster announced, in confident and reassuring tones, as if we would be pleased to hear it, that there was a Crisis. I forget which one it was: someone had robbed us of a colony, or the miners had gone on strike, or the balance of payments was adrift. Nonetheless, it was clear that the news greatly cheered my fellow-passengers, many of whom had gone for months or years without a decent Crisis. A natural aroma, a mood, began to take shape: that distinctive British mood of confidence in eternal values and rightness, coupled with a feeling of endless decline and decay, that we have in fact been living in for the last twenty-five years. We all got off the ship at Southampton, where the customs men went through the luggage hunting for illicit copies of *Lady Chatterley's Lover*; then we stepped out into the ancient land. It looked much as it always had, if not more so. The houses, the trains, even the people, appeared very tiny. People stood on street corners, talking in hushed tones about the bad weather. There was no Piggly Wiggly, and life was sedate. Everything was as one had always expected – or was it?

For, riding up to London on the tiny train, filled with silent, self-questioning people, it seemed that certain things were in fact changing, probably for good. The agrarian past, for example, was disappearing very rapidly. The Electricity Board vans were out everywhere, cutting down all the trees they could see; speculative builders were busy all over, raping the land and putting up squashed-together houses for toy people to live in. A concept of the modern seemed to have overtaken the British, here and there. Suburban dwellers were adding sun-lounges to the backs of their semi-detacheds; there were plastic-covered urinals, mosaic-fronted tobacconists, cedar-wood bicycle sheds. In London this uncharacteristic taste for the modern and the new was even more apparent. The beehive hairdo and the glass-walled office block spoke word of a new regime. Shops in Marks and Spencer's international style were going up apace. In the streets, there was a lot of youth about, asserting youthiness. In the shops, Swedish glass and Danish furniture indicated that the British were acceding to what the experts in these things – and now, suddenly, Britain was filled with experts in such things, calling them sociologists – called cultural drag. Commercial television had started, and the jingle-writers were showing off their wares, the pop-stars screeching in mid-atlantic accents. There were super-markets instead of grocers' shops; a kind of inebriated torpor, the kind of glazed look that comes to people's eyes after they have been watching too many television quiz shows, seemed to have settled over the population. Austerity had stopped, growth was growing, and the droop-moustached Prime Minister of the day was saying we had all 'never had it so good'. As someone put it at the time, the British were replacing the jingoism of the past with the bingoism of the present. Everywhere people were worrying about just the same kind of problems that had been disturbing Americans – the problem of conformity, the perils of creeping subur-banization, the woes of the waist-high culture, the spirit of the shook-up generation. It was apparent that I had re-turned at a time of subtle transformation. It was not that the old English stuffiness had gone away; it was there, more than ever. But at the same time the British were turning themselves into a nation of modern consumers, on the world model, aligning the old mood of post-imperial tristesse with the new mood of Having It Good.

I have told you all this because there are phases in the lives of writers when certain essential materials seem to drop before them, all ready to be used. I came back home just at the time when my provincial redbrick novel was, after all, being published: I was all ready to begin. And it was about all this, America and England, post-imperial tristesse and the new English unease, that I wanted to write. Just at this same time, my old colleague and mentor, Michael Orsler, bearded now and wearing glinting spectacles, had also returned from a stint aboard. He had been teaching in Singapore and Hong Kong, and become known as Master of Manners to a thousand Chinese schoolchildren. Comparing notes, we decided that we had come home again at a curious tidal moment, a cross-over point in British history. What to do about it? Humour, I thought, in the circumstances, seemed the only answer. I began an American novel, and also, in a frenzy of invention, started writing a number of humorous articles for magazines on both sides of the Atlantic. Developing from these articles – in *Vogue*, the *New Yorker*, *Harper's Magazine*, and *The Atlantic Monthly* in the States, and in *Punch* and the *Tatler* in Britain (to the editors and proprietors of all of which warm acknowledgements are due for permission to reprint) – came two humorous books, which fattened a selected number of Christmas stockings in 1960 and 1962. One of these books was called *Phogey! How to Have Class in a Classless Society*, and the other *All Dressed Up and Nowhere To Go, or The Poor Man's Guide to the Affluent Society*. It is these two books, revised to fit neatly into one, and with some but not all of the period allusions removed, that you are now about to enter.

I am glad to see them in print again because they do draw together so much of the experience and material that started me off as a writer. It is all long ago; the world is no longer so young, and nor for that matter am I. We do have *Dallas* and Legionnaire's disease, the Melamine tableware has long since been lost, and I do not any more wear clip-on bow ties. Instead of the age of You've Never Had It So Good, we have the new era of sado-monetarism, a little less of everything for everyone. Harder notes of satire in order; I shall be trying to oblige. So is all this a period piece? To a point, yes; but not entirely. For the ship on which we seem now to be sinking is the one that set sail in the 1950s, when I went to America, came back again, discovered the British divided between two worlds, and ventured on the analysis you are now poised to read. It is true that some of the things I then saw with amazement and described with surprise have become the routine, the ordinary, the commonplace stuff of British life. Matters have indeed been going rather oddly, this last twenty years or so. We've become a very strange lot of chaps altogether – wearing jeans in public, dressing ourselves in decorated and inscribed underwear, drinking aperitifs, reading paperback novels, listening through head-phones to the barbaric yawp of street-wise, green-haired mutants, as they sing their songs that complain that no one likes them simply because they chose to be so unlikeable, and fornicating to excess. Yes, change has come; but has all that, really, been *us*? The answer, surely, is surely not. Indeed it has taken only three Argentinians, hard men in hotel doormen's clothes, inflamed by the desire to assert their territorial rights over penguins, to reveal to us that, beneath the logo-ed T-shirts and the supporters' scarves, the jogging knickers and the ra-ra skirts, we remain pretty much what we always were: bold, decent, nineteenth-century, unmistakably right and, in a word, British to the core. The surface may have changed, but, somewhere down in the subterranean currents where we keep what chaps used to call our souls, the old national self goes soldiering on, ready to emerge whenever Crisis calls, as Crisis, in the end, always does. But, if we are to face it properly, advice is called for. Which is why, at this very moment, we have such need of the book that follows.

MALCOLM BRADBURY
Norwich, 1982

CONTENTS

PREFACE

Many writers have observed that returning home to England, after a long spell abroad, is an *ordeal*; there is something about England, a sort of perpetual spiritual fog, a pervasive provinciality, a leisureliness about life, a difficulty about getting things done, a certain sanctimonious sense that England is the centre of the universe, an orderliness, a neatness, a smallness, a nineteenth-centuryness . . . these things, and more, create an aroma and a mood. It is a sticky mood – life here seems so much harder, just to do it. There is little deference to comfort and ease, too much deference to authority. There are a lot of dogs. Shops say: Established in 1748. People say: It can't be done. Though the horse has virtually disappeared, roads are built, and clothes are designed, as if it still had sovereignty. George Orwell, discussing the different air of England, pointed to the essential Englishness of suet puddings, bad teeth and red pillar boxes, but one could pick almost anything – the multiplicity of electric plug sizes, for instance (where else in the civilized world could you go into fifty houses and not find one in which the plug on a newly purchased iron fitted?) or the notices on toilet paper that say PLEASE WASH YOUR HANDS, or the radio voice that says 'It is very nearlah twelve and a half minutes past nine'. This is the adjunct; what is the essence?

By a curious coincidence, the author and a friend, Orsler by name, returned to England at the same time from vastly different parts of the globe. Spry, debonair, well-dressed Malcolm Bradbury had newly come from the United States; bespectacled, large-eared Michael Orsler had come from the Orient which, we may be sure, was not for him inscrutable.

We returned at the time of a general election, when one party was declaring, 'You've never had it so good', and another cried, 'You can have it even better'. Things seemed to be changing; many people had bought motor cars, to keep in their garages until roads had been built to accommodate them; the middle classes, once the guardians of propriety, had become illegal, because of income tax and motoring offences and because it was now in style to be working class; the first road to be built in England since the Romans left was shortly to be opened, and people were planning camping trips to the roadside to watch cars going by, and to drop cigarette packets on to them from overpasses. But it did not take us long to see that beneath this veneer of alteration, things were as they had always been – if not more so.

One tasted England from the moment one boarded ship. What was it? The thirties décor described in the brochures as 'modern', with its panels of inlaid wood, its lighting so indirect that when it went wrong no one could find it, its cubist armchairs, now well-packed with dust, in which the tendons were stretched alarmingly? Was it the green basket chairs in the Winter Garden Lounge, which left patterns on the skin which weeks of scrubbing could not quite efface? Was it the teashop trio that played there (Wilf on wiolin, Untidy Bert on pianner and Reggie on double bass) who, after clomping about a bit before starting (fearing for an audience), performed 'Tiptoe through the Tulips' and 'Daffodil Lullaby' to a missionary reading *Exodus* and an assemblage of enfantele, consumed with curiosity, while waiters came round with tea and rubber fruit cakes? Was it the stewards, largely fuddy-duddies who had, twenty years ago, retired from watching over-stuffed animals in Kensington museums, men with far-away eyes, blood-pressured cheeks, London club pates with fringes of whitish monk-hair, and lips like red rubber tubing?

One was struck, too, by the way in which the English fell into postures of command or submission, whether they needed to or not. Travelling home on an English liner, after a year of the social permissiveness of America, I noticed a curious fact. All the places at dinner were reserved; moreover, it was a reputable line and there was little doubt but that the meal would be served. Nonetheless, half an hour before the dinner gong sounded, a long, quiet and orderly queue of British persons began to form in front of the closed doors of the dining-room, straggling thence throughout the bowels of the ship, and rendering access to cabins and lavatories difficult. Nothing would disturb this placid line – not the fact that its members were persistently asked by stewards to disband, nor the fact that foreigners, wanting in ingrained decency, habitually walked past the queue (which politely advanced at the pace of its oldest and slowest members) once the dining-room doors were opened. The line became a positive embarrassment to the whole ship, which, toward mealtimes, would markedly tilt and begin to circle. Even when this was pointed out, the queue refused to disperse, and eventually became twice as long – for the foreigners joined it.

Likewise, I tried to purchase, aboard the same vessel, a fountain pen, and I asked the English girl who administered the shop whether I might try some pens. 'Sorry, sir, I can't spend all my day wiping fountain pen nibs clean,' said the girl; and suddenly, as I borrowed someone's pencil, there stirred in my mind a harmonious and beautiful understanding, suddenly I was in England again, suddenly I knew why so many Americans I had met (broad-minded Americans who, fearless in the face of the notorious European lack of hygiene, had actually *been* to England) had been under the impression that England was an island of ceaseless fog and drizzle. They thought it foggy, I suddenly realized, because, to the spirit, it seemed like it.

Some little time later, I was comparing notes with Orsler in the comfort of a Suffolk public house. Orsler, then (as now) a rumbustious and guffawing youth, sensitive withal to racial characteristics, confirmed my observations and added his own. Returning from the Orient, he had noted masters of plantations quail before stewards once aboard ship. 'Everything we wanted, even if it was legitimate, we were made ashamed of wanting, even if it was available. We wanted coffee. I pressed The Bell. The Steward came in, smelling: "Was it you who rung?"

'"We'd like coffee," I said.

'"No coffee at this hour," he said, "Coffee is served each night after dinner."

'I started to protest. "Now, what would you like?" he asked, "I haven't got all . . ."

'"I'll have a beer," I said smartly, "Tomato juice for my wife. Fresh orange juice for the baby."

'"No fresh fruit at the moment," said the steward.

'"Make it fizz," I said.

'"No tomato juice," said the steward. "That'll be one and four."

'"May I sign?" I asked.

'"No," he said. "We don't encourage passengers."

'"Oh," I said.'

Orsler paused for a moment, with an intimate smile of recollection lighting his rubicund features, owlish in their glasses, and then he commented:

'People say you really know you're back in England when you get off the boat and see how small everything is – the cars, the goods trains, the houses. But that's not it. It's when, as I did, you rush to the booking office and try to get a ticket, and there are two minutes before your train leaves, and there are twenty people waiting at the L to M window, so you go to the M to O window and ask for a ticket to London. You can see porters closing all the doors on the train, and men throwing the last fragile parcel violently into the brake van. The booking clerk, with his bottom against the stove, says: "Next window." You say: "But there are twenty people at the next window and the train's just going." And he says: "Well, it can't be 'elped, can it?" That's it, the home that raised us.'

We agreed; and I remarked that the English supposed that one only went abroad because one had to and returned as soon as one could. We were interrupted in this thought by an old countryman who, to our certain knowledge, had never in his life been more than five miles away from the village, and this only to go to the market town to buy new yorks to put round the knees of his corduroys. Nevertheless, 'Back home again, eh, bor?' he cried. 'Ah, you got to go a long way to beat ole England, eh?' This set up a train of thought which culminated in the concept of *phogey*, a concept to define that phase of the English mind in which the artificial stands superior to the real, the traditional to the new, the mannered to the frank – that stout spirit of British phlegm which maintains protocol, and pooh-poohing, rudeness and possessiveness, provinciality and superiority, and makes living in England like walking through syrup. The phogey is half fogey, half phoney – phoney because there is a whole tradition and structure of pretence in him. After all, in the modern world, one does not have to be a phogey – one chooses to be. Add a touch of the word foggy and you have our meaning. Thus this is a *new* phenomenon (it was natural to be nineteenth-century in the nineteenth century, but it takes hard work to be so in the twentieth) and a NEW CONCEPT. Of course, it will quickly pass current as what was always known.

For the phogey is the man who, living in what the Americans call 'the modern world of today', wishes really that it were yesterday and contrives to pretend that it is. Social change has taken place; some of it he approves of, some of it he complains of, and most of it he ignores. He thinks that things are as they always were; and he has institutions that make it seem so. The primary institution, the one that preserves all the others, is, of course, class. The classless society may be here; but nobody knows about it. People go on having class in the old, well-tried way. It is there, at the heart of us all, and we have all made sure of our own way of having class in a classless society. For the phogey believes in authority. The English, unlike the Americans (who think a plumber the equal of a university professor), are masters of deference, artists, too, at putting people in their places. And knowing one's place, whatever it is, is the essential English gift; it comes from an ancient sense of order and a faith that one's own place, whatever it is, has been worth getting to. Authoritarianism by consent is a sound British principle, which is why people are happy to stand in line at bus-stops, or call their bosses 'guv'. This is the famous British politeness, used by that race to be rude with to other people. Yet change had come, the world was not the same; the signs of doubt and disorientation were already evident. How, then, would the British cope with it?

'It needs, of course, a book,' said Orsler. 'Two,' I said, and undertook to oblige. We agreed that such a book could not evade – however improper it might be to speak of it – the subject of class, and how to have it in this changing world. (For, suspicious though we may be, there is undoubtedly something in all of us that yearns for the safety and stability of it all.) Thus came the following – an attempt to assist those who, in the new time of flux, might, for the first time ever, be feeling the need for assistance and guidance. So here is a book for the new uncertainty, a book that will assist those who want more class to have it, and those who do not to find a path through the new affluence that besets us. I did consult, as one does these days, a sociologist or two: and I am grateful to Bryan Wilson and Howard Higman for many felicitous suggestions. But above all I am grateful to the dedicatee, Orsler himself, without whom, one suspects, the fifties would never have been understood at all.

PART ONE

PHOGEY!

One of the things that we English like to tell foreigners (if we speak to them at all) is that our society is democratic; but how miserable we should all be if it were. We do, in this country, affirm the principle that Everyone's Opinion Is as Good as Anyone Else's; our qualification is that some people need to be told what are the best opinions to have. The difference between the English and American patterns of democracy can be simply summed up; while America is broadly speaking a permissive society, England is authoritarian, by consent. Visiting Americans always notice how easily we fall into postures of command or submission. We are dragooned in teashops, post offices, buses, by people who have, always, something better to do, and say so. Likewise we are dragooned by our government, the Inland Revenue, the National Health Service. The reason that we accept it is that it seems to us always to have been like that, and if it always was, it must be right.

As Freud ('that psychology nonsense') would say, we are looking for our fathers or, alternatively, for our sons – because, in matters of authority, it takes, as with the tango, two to do it (a phogeyarch and phogeysite, let us call them). In fact neither is lost for long. Observe our respect for law and order, our desire not to cause trouble, our fondness for keeping ourselves to ourselves, our lack of complaint when we are obviously being lied to, or cheated. And indeed how else can one explain the fact that retired army generals are considered natural choices for the high management posts in nationalized industry – and the even stranger fact that retired railwaymen are almost never made generals? It is all, of course, because army generals are trained in authoritarianism. Why can't we be like the Americans, and put our generals in positions where they can do no harm whatsoever – like the Presidency?

Democracy affirms that all men are rightly equal, and equally right. Since this is manifestly untrue, and since certain things are plainly and by divine plan morally right and others morally wrong, the phogey is in a firm position. Thus it is morally right that drain-pipes should be on the outside of houses. *I was there* when an American asked an Englishman: 'But why do you have your drain-pipes on the *outside* of your houses?' 'Well, obviously,' said the Englishman, with, in our direction, that amused smile that people have when they are asked silly questions, 'so that we can get at them more easily when they freeze.' (I do not deny the grain of truth here; English houses are so badly heated, by the same divine law, that the pipes might very well freeze indoors as well; after all, comfort isn't everything, and if bedrooms were not cold in England there'd probably be no sex here at all.)

Whence springs the phogey mentality? It doubtless derives from the ancient picture of the Englishman, that national character which is the product of history, or rather, what phogeys have taught, and learned, as history. Summarizing this stock figure's virtues and vices, we get something like this:

(a) STIFF UPPER LIPPERY, or steadiness under fire. Bertrand Russell says that people imitate their national heroes, and surely Drake was ours. The scholar was hero to the old Chinese; this could not happen in England.

(b) NON-OSTENTATION. What the English most dislike about the Americans is their celebration of their skills. Englishmen, never seeming to enjoy anything, never display either their talents or their wealth. English guidebooks say: 'Looking above your head, you will see a somewhat imperfect hammerbeam roof, marred by the fact that the chimney is placed somewhat to the left of where it should be. There are far better examples of this type of architecture at . . .' It is a proper modesty and since the other places cited are usually too far away to reach (since there are, in England, no roads), it costs nothing. In America, though, it would always be the best, and perfect. This attitude depends, of course, on the other persons present being informed enough to disagree with you. It has its roots, one suspects, in the conditions of the early nineteenth century, when the only way for the rich to avoid social revolution was to make it seem that it was enjoyable to be poor.

(c) SELECTIVE IGNORANCE. This is the theory that there are certain things it is better not to know. Most of these things are foreign anyway. The argument leads of course to an empirical view of the universe – try what was done before and, if it doesn't work, muddle through. The world is full of information, but most of it the British prefer to ignore. Associated with this view is the notion of the gentleman amateur, who is not expert at anything, but contrives, when necessary, to know people who are.

(d) SUPERIORITY TO FOREIGNERS. This is because, once, we were. It is now impossible for an Englishman to believe that Americans have a superior material standard of life, or that Russia has a superior educational system, any more than it is possible for him to believe that women are intelligent.

(e) MUDDLING THROUGH. The twentieth century has done some strange things to England. Of course, it has not got off scot-free; England has done some strange things to the twentieth century. Yet somehow the new age has made its mark; it may even be making us adaptable. But we doubt it. Muddling through once did ring true, and was part of a Victorian modesty which cloaked flexibility, initiative and the capacity for brilliant improvisation. The fact now is that the new industrial age is upon us, and it requires planning; and planning is suspect, because THEY plan. So we continue to muddle through. Consider that in England there are no roads.* The real reason why England has been proof against invasion for so long is that it is impossible to get inland. There are only lanes, clogged with motionless traffic and blocked by herds of cows wandering home to be milked. In any case, if invaders did land, they would never get anywhere, because no one knows where anywhere is. They would ask their way of old men and be misdirected, or told: 'If I was you I wouldn't start from here.' Frustrated and muddled, they would go back where they came from, leaving a dotard or two to speculate in the village snug about the snow on their boots.

These cannot be said to be undesirable traits. But since physical courage is now outmoded (there are no more victories), modesty inhibiting, ignorance fatal, superiority dangerous, and muddling through completely ineffectual, the British have responded to the challenge with their usual phlegm; in adversity, the traits have become *heightened*. Being improved by adversity is in fact

(f) THE LAST TRAIT, and much the most important. An Englishman arranges systems of manners and institutions which are, to him, unchallengeable. He admits there are two sides to every question (his, and one that no right-thinking person in full possession of his senses could possibly hold) and yet he will maintain for ever that certain things are manifestly true. This is the essence of phogey. The phogey is the man who maintains his equilibrium, under all circumstances, by the use of *protocol*. For the phogey, there are no new situations; everything has happened before. He is concerned with Institutionalizing Things, and Living by Rote. He depends on a *voluntary* authoritarian structure in which everyone knows his place, from high to low, and per-

*There is now one, but it stops before it gets there.

ceives this condition as essentially unchangeable; it was *God* who pointed out that, with tea, some social classes put milk in first, and others last, and that one way is *inherently* better than another.

Yes, there are certain characteristics of the English spirit which occur in both reactionaries and radicals, and make Englishmen different from any other race of men anywhere else on earth. It is in these residual, permanently nineteenth-century qualities that our society maintains itself; and herein lies *phogey*.

*

'Our car costs so much to run now, we live in it.' Things are in a pretty pass, I found, talking to the m.c. (middle class) young phogey whose comments culminated in the above admission; the old pretences are increasingly hard to keep up. The phogey is, to some extent, at bay. This is inevitable, of course; it is increasingly difficult, in this age of equality and relativism, to convey even *valid* notions of superiority. The phogey is oriented to values that no longer survive in their pure state. Essentially inner-directed and tradition-bound, he is the product of a society tooled up, so to speak, for Empire building. The building, however, has stopped, and he has no real place to exercise his talents. One foresees the end of all this in some small colony named, let us say, Umbala, in the heart of Africa. It is the last surviving colony and here they are all gathered – the hundreds of governors and the thousands of administrators, packed together in a few square miles, clutching the Colonial Office set of Kipling, governing and administrating each other and dressing each night for dinner. A sad but likely resolution.

The phogey's values are inculcated in him from an early age, by his nanny or his public school or even his elementary (in phogey schools you sit on straight-backed chairs, good for the spine, and on wooden benches, chastening to the rump, and you play team games, because there is something *moral* about rugger). The author can remember the days when schools were grim buildings, with few toilets, and self-expression and finger painting had never been heard of. However, the Dewey-eyed system of permissive education, where children learn how to have well-rounded personalities and get on well with the group, has never caught on in England, and one doubts if it ever will. Phogeys have ill-rounded personalities and are proud of it; they suspect that people who get on well at parties and can Influence Friends and Make People are up to no good; they are usually right. The true phogey, in any case, has nothing to celebrate, and is much more at home at a funeral than at a party.

The phogey spends his life testing the universe against English institutions and if it isn't somehow right, he asks for something to be done about it; after all, obviously, God is English. These days, it is less easy to convince foreigners that England is the centre of the world (because it isn't) and that to behave in ways unlike the English is an aberration. The fact is that foreigners are learning that you get by more easily if you are less like the English, for the phogey, being stringently moral, lacks fluidity. Understand, I am not saying anything against foreigners; some of my best friends are foreigners and remember – they have not had our advantages.

The phogey is, then, Phineas Fogg; he expects foreign climes to give him special dispensation; Englishmen go out in the midday sun in the firm knowledge that, in a day or two, the sun will *catch on*. Climbing a very high mountain in remote America with an English phogey girl, author Bradbury was not surprised to hear her say, when they reached the top, sucking hard for oxygen, while black specks hovered menacingly in the sky above them, and nature seemed red in tooth and claw: 'Looook, I say, look at that bird; isn't that an English blackbird?' Cut off from Ovaltine, life in America had been a hard fight for her, but with the stout English capacity for transmogrifying all American situations (and birds) into English ones, she had not felt the pinch at all. (The same girl once accompanied the same Bradbury to the film of *Lady Chatterley's Lover*, and at the point where Lady Chatterley's head — all of her that was visible on screen — was expressing the highest access of bliss at what had happened to her when she and the gamekeeper had been caught by a rainstorm in a secluded hut, the girl turned with a distraught expression on her face: 'Her horse is getting wet,' she said.)

Phogey values come completely from inside, and are internalized by the age of eleven. Americans change their characters with their clothes, and whenever they go from one room to another; they will join a discussion condemning dirty jokes, go through a door, and tell dirty jokes. Phogeys are stuck with their characters all the time, and like it. Americans believe in being nice, and they do it by being whatever the majority of people want them to be; their view of character is that it's a nice place to visit but you wouldn't want to live there. Phogeys dislike being nice, in case they are nice to someone who doesn't deserve it. And, as the phogey says, if you are odious, why lie about it? Ask Americans what they believe in, and they say: 'It depends who I'm with.' English people don't care whom they are with, and prefer not to be, anyway.

A nineteenth-century figure, then, the phogey survives into the twentieth and finds that his code no longer quite fits, and that people are doing things in other ways and getting away with it, even though it must be apparent that his way is best. The phogey is inner-directed — which means doing unto others because they did it unto you; and in these days of relativism, when you can't blame anyone for anything because it was the fault of his environment or his toilet-training, the inner-directed man is an anachronism. Inner-directed people make fine generals, managing directors and sado-masochists; they depend, however, on a society in which one code of values is universal. In short, they need no public relations men, because who needs relations with the public anyway? English government and American government is much the same, but the Americans explain why they do what they do; and this gives the public the illusion that they can interfere.

'We're bringing up Garth to be inner-directed,' an American academic couple explained to me one day, when I found them flogging their child, in a most un-American way, with a carpet-beater. 'The next generation's going to need a few of them.' But this is no good, for if you don't have a phogey-speaking society there's nothing you can do. 'It's no use,' I told this couple, 'if you're going to understand him as well.' They looked upset. 'The trouble is, we understand him already. We wouldn't have if we'd known . . . but well, I guess once you've read Spock you've read Spock, and that's all there is to it.' Other-direction is bringing up your children to be happy; in inner-directed England happiness is looked upon, quite properly, with universal distrust. I take these two categories from an American sociologist named David Riesman, who in his book *The Lonely Crowd* defined the two life-styles in order that people could choose which brand they preferred. To sum it up simply, the difference between them is this; the inner-directed man says, 'I don't know anything about art, but I know what I like,' while the other-directed man says: 'I know all about art, but I don't know what I like.' With other-directed persons, you can never get through a door, because they all want to go through it last.

Think of Etonians. When you meet an Etonian in the street, you walking in one direction, he walking in the other, you will stop (if he cares to recognize you) and chat, and he will take you by the arm and you will walk on, chatting, both in the direction in which he was going; it can take you as much as half an hour to get away, by which time you are probably a good bus-ride out of your route. This is inner-direction, and is, to the phogey, as important as inner cleanliness. There are certain inherent truths about the universe which the phogey takes for granted, as common to all men, or all who matter. One, for example, is that everyone who needs to know knows where the Athenaeum is, so that it is wholly unnecessary to label it.

Visitors run into this difficulty constantly; thus, 'It's a wonder she didn't call a bobby,' said an American, describing a misadventure in an English fishmonger's, when he went in to ask for some of the snails in the window. 'There are,' said the girl indignantly, 'no snails in *our* shop.' Aware that he had stepped on an obscure English prejudice, the American went carefully. 'Snails to eat,' he said. 'People don't eat snails,' said the girl with a laugh. 'In France . . .' 'Oh,' said the girl, 'don't talk to me about *France*. You can't even find a clean toilet . . .' 'Then what do you call those things over there?' asked the American. 'They're winkles,' said the girl. 'Can I have some?' asked the American. 'They're not snails, you know,' said the girl. 'That's all right,' said the American. 'Those *happen*,' said the girl, 'to come out of the *sea*.' 'I'd like some,' said the American. 'What do you want them for?' asked the girl. 'To eat,' said the American, and he added, too casually, 'tell me – how do you eat these winkles?' 'Well, how *do* people eat winkles?' cried the girl. 'I don't know,' admitted the American. 'How do you think?' cried the girl, 'With a pin, of course.' 'Of course,' said the American.

By inner-directedness we mean that the phogey is a man with a response to situations that don't even *exist* yet. This is because he will not admit the principle of change. All situations are commonplaces and the phogey lives by sleep-walking; thus in railway carriages a dry clearing of the throat and a piercing stare and slight re-arrangement of clothing will suffice for any eventuality, from complaints about smoking, down to persons who want to talk. I have been in railway carriages with phogeys and tried to tell them that their clothes are on fire ('I say, I believe your clothes are on fire') only to be withered by this treatment, so that I sat there uneasily while the man's clothing smouldered all the way to Crewe. It seemed heartless, but I knew he would have wanted it that way. The symptoms of the sleepwalking manner are broadly those of drunkenness – loss of critical faculty and a sense of cosiness (*gemütlich*). It is the mood of the completely self-centred and assured, confident that things are always as they were. Observe a phogey faced, for the *first time*, by one of those contemporary chairs into which you insert your bum deeply and then, as it were, peer out over your kneecaps to spy out the land; he will find it absurd. He will find modern poetry absurd, and modern art. He cannot understand why people are not writing good poetry, like that fellow Tennyson, who really understood tears, idle tears, and why Edward Marsh ever stopped publishing *Georgian Poetry*. Yet notice the young phogey who has grown up with the new. He will not find the contemporaneous ridiculous (contemporary furnishing, which is in fact ten years out of date, is a phogey style; however, the idea behind it, that articles can be appreciated SIMULTANEOUSLY with their creation, is new and anti-phogey) – but he *will* be amused, like Gilbert Pinfold, by things that are changed during his own lifetime. Thus to the phogey things are starting to go wrong just around now. Phogeys are not makers, and chart no new ways; they are too involved with the old ones, and know them to be right.

For phogeys are the instruments of tradition. (Tradition is a key phogey word, and here is how tradition works: 'The Manor and most of the soil are the property of Captain Philip Bennett, MP, of *Rougham Hall*, a handsome castel-lated Tudor Mansion which was erected by his father.' *History, Gazetteer and Directory of Suffolk*.) Tradition is also Joe Higgs, seconded from his dustcart during the summer months in order to act as town-crier for the American tourists. The phogey's survival depends on the extent to which inherited manners and conventions remain unchallenged from outside. But his solidified tradition is in fact a recent one, and phogeyness a recent phenomenon, characteristic of a late stage in society when institutionalization and emphasis on manners become substitutes for active adjustments to new conditions. This is known as taking the long view, and depends on the doubtful proposition that the world will, at some point, take up again where it left off in 1914, and the sun will come out again. Phogeys hark back, back to the Good Old Days. This is a phrase used by phogeys without thought, because old days were all good, much gooder than the days they try to fob people off with now. You could have a good meal at the Savoy and a girl for the night, and still get change out of a bob, whatever that might be. Even working-class life was better; people starved, but they enjoyed it much more than they do now. British summers were always long and hot and filled with cucumber sandwiches; indeed it is quite clear that it is climatic change that has made the twentieth century since 1914 the miserable and chaotic affair it has so obviously been. And all this is why the favourite British sport is archaeology, a form of extended reminiscence, and why the high point of British sentiment is a garden with a *sundial* in it.

And so, the phogey tells us, 'In my opinion all human affairs get worse as time goes on.' From his point of view this is true, and it is not an entirely improper view of history to take, given what history gives us in return. Hence people who get involved with things like change are by definition unreliable; and the phogey naturally distrusts the young, and intellectuals, because they are principles of enquiry, and people who enquire about things tend to be articulate. And articulate is one thing phogeys are not. After all, there is little to articulate about, because one knows instinctively when things are as they should be. The way you know this is by *experience*, which is what the young and the intellectuals do not have. 'I think one of the purposes of us old fogeys in life is to stop the young from being silly,' said one phogey MP lately, representing a large constituency. 'When I was young. . . ,' says the old phogey; when he was young he was, of course, a young phogey, a class of which there is never any lack. Faced by the mysterious phenomenon of the 'Angry Young Men', a new young phogey, a Mr Plantagenet

Somerset Fry, spoke up for young phogeys everywhere: 'Frankly, the "angry young man" never cut any ice at all, and it is ignored rather than reviled, as it ought to be in London.' Clearly what was so irritating about the angry young men was not that they were angry but that they were *young*; it is, after all, the old who are entitled to be angry. And it must be said that there is quite a lot of phogey even in the angry young men themselves – angry, after all, either because their fathers were not at Oxford, or because they were; angry, too, both because their protest was not understood, and because it was so immediately accepted. Not by everyone, of course: Mr Christopher Sykes, who is 'tall, broad, ebulliently aristocratic in manner,' says the press, accused them of being full of belly-aching and self-pity. But it could be, it could just possibly be, that it is the phogey spirit that has made them so.

*

Phogeys are of all age-groups, all social classes, all political and religious persuasions, all sexes. They can equally be top people who read the *Daily Sketch* (once you get to the top, you can stop reading *The Times*; that chore is over) and go beagling; or lib-labs who live on wheat germ and have petitions to sign whenever you go and see them. What they all possess is assurance, the assurance that they are superior to, or inferior to, someone else.

Let us note some of the characteristics of the phogey, that he be recognized. Throughout society he is ubiquitous, from the henna-haired harridans in teashops, for whom customers are an imposition, to those at the top – the Phogeyarchs, let us call them, in official power positions (members of Watch Committees, Lord Chamberlains, Hanging Judges, Diplomats, Dons, Scoutmasters, Youth Leaders, and the like). Below the phogeyarchs and existing in far greater numbers are the phogeysites. While the former is a phogey because he is in a phogey job, and is known to be such even before he acts or speaks, the latter have to work for years to attain general recognition. By their indifference to their fellows and their insistence on the letter (no juniors in the senior men's washroom) they are marked. Their long wait has often made them morose . . . and afraid. Always they are careful but *are they careful enough*?

Phogeys are proper, orderly and well-mannered. 'There should be a law . . .' says the phogey. Actually there almost always is. The Americans distrust and resent their policemen; the English respect theirs, because they know they are looking after them. There is a story told of the philosopher T. E. Hulme, which shows how this respect is returned. Hulme was found by a policeman one night in Soho Square, urinating against a tree. 'You'll have to move on, sir,' said the policeman. Hulme protested, 'But I'm a member of the middle classes.' 'I'm sorry, sir,' said the policeman, retiring in embarrassment.

The English treat life as they do their washrooms; they believe that you should leave society as you would wish to find it. For this reason even the most revolutionary persons cannot conceive of too much change, nor of fighting for it if it is going to disturb people. When people suggest change in England, the reply is always: 'It wouldn't work.' Phogeydom is thus preserved by law and institutions even as it withers away in persons. This is in the cause of order and control, two principles of phogey *gemütlichkeit*, which holds that life is really nice, if you did but know it. Much of the famed English tolerance and respect for persons is because it's too much trouble to go on about the thing. Argument only exposes the divisions. The thing to do is to shut one's eyes. Thus many of the hostilities implicit in society are hidden in institutions that conceal behind an apparent relationship a fundamental indifference, or antipathy, or class-hostility on either side. The great English kewing system is just such a pretence, as in this example:

BUS CONDUCTOR (*collecting fares*): Kew? Kew?
PASSENGER: Thrupny, please.
BUS CONDUCTOR: Kew (*Taking money.*) Kew.
PASSENGER: Kew.
CONDUCTOR (*handing ticket*): Kew.
PASSENGER: Kew.
CONDUCTOR (*handing change*): Kew.
PASSENGER: Kew.
CONDUCTOR: Kew. (*Going on down bus.*) Kew? Kew?

This is made even more difficult if the passenger is going to Kew. This is pervasive politeness, and the present author was able to score as many as fifteen kews in the course of one transaction, the purchase of a packet of cigarettes.

'You are liable . . .' say the phogey notices; is there anywhere in the world where you are liable for so much, so often? Nowadays there are so many traffic police that motorists have to go about in pairs; and government by notice is rife – NO DANCING, NO SINGING, NO GRINNING. The story is even recorded of a notice, a phogey notice, which said: DO NOT THROW STONES AT THIS NOTICE. One young phogey of my acquaintance was driving through Bury St. Edmunds where he lives and *keeps a diary*, when his car licence became unstuck from the windscreen. Rather than offend, he drove with one hand and held it up to view with the other. People ran for cover as he zig-zagged down the street. 'You're liable, you know,' he said. It is my contention that if he had hit someone and been taken to court, he would have got off because he was obeying the law.

And every Englishman knows the feeling of guilt that washes over him when he has trespassed against some institution, even when it is some petty sin like having used it while the train was standing in the station or stamping on the top deck of a Nottingham bus. (DRIVER BELOW: PLEASE DO NOT STAMP FEET, say the notices. Nottingham residents are lucky in having, as far as we know, the only city council go-ahead enough to clamp down on the great foot-stamping menace, even though, in this case as with so many others, no one would have thought of the offence, until the notice suggested it.) The author and his friend Orsler were once caught together in a guilt-situation of this kind; it was unauthorized pea-shelling. They were caught by a guard in a railway train at Dawlish, shelling peas in preparation for their dinner that evening. Though they were creating no litter (Orsler, ever meticulous, was actually swallowing the empty shells) and there was no law against it, it was apparent enough that this was morally wrong and that, unless something were done about it, pea-podding might run rife on British Railways. Therefore with supreme aplomb, 'Sorry, sir, no pea-podding,' said the guard. In such a situation, how deep the soul is seared. And that is *it*, the phogey in all of us.

One of the classic forms of phogeydom is the phogey pooh-pooh. In America, when an idea is suggested, people criticize the person who suggested it but then set about trying to do it; in England, when an idea is suggested, people praise the person who suggested it, regarding him as a useful man to have around, but never do anything about it. Americans do not like people who have ideas, because it's hostile to the group (if one has an idea, one never says, as in Europe, 'I happen to be an expert on this . . .'; one says, 'Well, I don't know anything about this, and this is just off the top of my head, but let's put this one out on the step and see if the cat licks it . . .'); however, they do tend to use the ideas. In England it is possible to get to the top by having ideas that no one has ever done anything about. Americans are pragmatists, and the great American phrase is 'So what?' — meaning all right, it's an idea, but what can you do with it?

In England the phogey pooh-pooh works like this. Let us suppose that a weekend trip to Scotland has been suggested, or the building of a garage: the English reply is, 'Good idea, old boy, but can't be done. Who'll look after the cat?' or 'Splendid thought, but we don't know enough about alignment, do we?' An Englishman's first response to any suggestion is that it cannot, in any circumstances, be done. Like *the* regulations ('Passengers are not allowed to stand if there are more than seven seats in the vehicle immediately following, in which case not more than four passengers are allowed to sit with the driver'), the phogey pooh-pooh adds to the strange sense of perpetual fog that one has in England. 'Sorry, sir, the bar's closed'; 'Sorry, sir, no eating in the library'; 'Sorry, can't sweep a chimney under six months.'

One of the illuminating differences between England and America lies in the words used to describe the service that in America is called INFORMATION and in England is called ENQUIRIES. The English notice is descriptive of the people on one side of the counter, the American of those on the other. In England, that is, you are entitled to *ask*; in America you are entitled to be *told*. These are two very different freedoms descriptive of two very different kinds of democracy. For while American democracy is going towards something, ours seems to be coming away from something.

As an Englishman, one only comes to understand the pooh-pooh when one has visited America or has been visited by Americans in England. Americans think that anything is possible; they are swiftly disabused when they visit the English shore.

Englishmen, with their sense of propriety and order, know that there are God-given laws that say that shops should close at six in the evening and that it is morally improper to drink beer in public places between three and six in the afternoon and after eleven at night; they know that most things are impossible and that there is nothing to be done about them. It is only when they have American guests and run out of potatoes at ten o'clock at night, or want to buy a toothbrush on a Sunday, when the shops are allowed, by law, to be open but are not allowed, by law, *to sell anything* (or perhaps, one thing, like toothpaste), that they realize that their lives are bounded by an intrinsic sense of the limitations of the world. Only an American would dream of running out of potatoes at night in England, or suppose that there is a mechanical solution to the problem of switching off your television set without rising from your chair. Thus Englishmen, like myself, go to America simply in order to be able to find a place to eat at two in the morning.

*

People are asking: who, what, *why* is phogey? I have spoken of certain characteristics in the English spirit that occur both in reactionaries and radicals, and make Englishmen different from any other race of men anywhere on the earth. It is in these residual, permanently nineteenth-century qualities that our society maintains itself. The English are proper, rude, possessive, orderly, stingy and superior.

Not enough has been written about English rudeness. The phogey has a special sense of what is polite, which roughly corresponds in other nations with what is rude. It depends upon a simple contention; everyone has his place and can be put into it. Sir Harold Nicolson has in his book *Good Behaviour* a charming passage on Dr Johnson, in which he remarks that he cannot, alas, exhibit this great and good man as an example of English civility. 'He was kind to his cat, "Hodge", and bought him oysters; he was kind to his strange assortment of dependants; he was wonderfully kind to children, servants and beggars. But he was not kind to his equals or his superiors.' One does not need to elaborate on the strangeness of a society in which civility is expressed by kindness to one's superiors. The British are also good at a kind of rudeness in which they affect to be totally unaware that they are being rude; this is characterized by the 'Hark at me! What am I saying?' approach, and is condescending. Sir Harold himself is uncivil to the Americans in the same book, on the grounds that 'although I have lived and travelled much in the United States, and although I account many Americans among my closest friends, I have not the arrogance to suppose that I understand them, in the sense that I understand the Athenians of 2500 BC'. To most Englishmen this would not seem rude; but it is, and most Americans would know it is.

Let us put it another way. The phogey is not nice. Americans are too nice, and they are nice to people who don't deserve it; the English are too rude, and they are rude to people who don't deserve it. (An exception proving the rule is the body of New York customs persons, undoubtedly the rudest set of people on earth.)

The phogey is stoical, and believes that people should be able to put up with anything – he himself recognizing that he is one of the things people have to put up with. He does not believe in happiness, and resents it in others, especially in Americans, who think of happiness as a human right, and have written it into their constitution. He believes, like the Anglo-Saxons, in endurance and patience. He is pessimistic, because the world is not his any more, and because he harks back to a golden age, when you could send a gunboat and *it went*. He believes that England will one day get back on the Gold Standard. He feels that change has gone further than it has and no one is more ready to deplore what has not yet happened.

He is also non-competitive, stingy, individualistic, anti-feminist, and afraid of his father. He is stingy because he is materialistic. The Americans, contrary to the popular view, are not materialistic, and the British are. Americans throw things away, but the English have attics full of bits of string, brown paper wrapping, old cans and toothbrushes and so on, on the grandmotherly principle that 'it might come in for something'. The attic is the most important room in the English house, comparable with the bedroom in France and the playroom in America. It is problem-solving. The English love property, and respect it, and put fences round it, and wash it and scrub it, and make it last. They love a car that is twenty years old better than one which is two years old, because it has been around longer, and has stored up more affection. It is almost one of the family. They speak of *my* car, and *my* house, and *my* dog and *my* wife; ownership is all, and these things are the signposts of life, the proof that you really exist and are what you are. In consequence nothing ever gets thrown away but is kept or used again; and the economy fails to expand. The American economy is founded on waste, on beer cans being thrown away and left to rust, on paper handkerchiefs and disposable cartons. The English wonder how they can be used again. It may be protested that America is a richer society; the truth is, of course, that it is richer because it throws things away. In America advertisers claim for their products, among other things, that it is easy to jettison them. A large part of American industry is given over to workers and machines making parts of products which are contingent – which are never used, but are cast into the waste paper basket or put down the Dispose-All. Americans will build houses and leave them after one year. An American likes to acquire money, since this is a mark of success; but equally he likes to give it away. All the American business man really needs is a briefcase and an airline ticket. Public giving is traditional. Unfortunately giving things away in America can be dangerous, as they may get to the wrong organizations; so there are now foundations in America which offer to give money away for benevolent Americans and make the promise that they will never hear of it again. One of the reasons why socialism is functional in England is that charity is a favour rather than a custom (the one exception was the upper class, who now need charity themselves). Thus the English, in condemning Americans for their materialism, define the American attitude in terms of what their own would be if they behaved like that; for materials are things that Americans work with, but the English possess.

On the other hand, the phogey is non-mechanical. He does not understand machinery and would be lost in an American kitchen. He is suspicious of gadgets – of electric shoe polishers and electric can openers. Americans have machines for everything because it would be more expensive to employ people. In England, this stage will come and the phogey will be at a loss; confronted with apparatus, he will go and hide. He is also anti-convenience. The Americans developed a kind of shirt called the button-down shirt; at some point in American history there was a great wind-menace among executives, when gales blew up their shirt-collars in their faces. Meeting the problem with typical American know-how, the Americans developed a shirt which had buttons on the fabric to which the collar points can be fixed. Though these shirts are immensely neat and do not need to be starched, they have never been taken up in England. The best example is, of course, the English heating system, which doesn't. All the heat of English coal fires goes up the chimney, and heats aeroplanes.

The phogey is modest. This is because he is simply not interested in discussing his accomplishments with other people, since they probably would not understand anyway. In any case accomplishments do not really matter, since they are only what you have *done*, not what you *are*; moreover, it is better to be a gentleman amateur than a specialist at anything, because specialists are *too serious*. Likewise the phogey is unenthusiastic. It was, I think, Sir John Squire who reviewed a book called *Entertainment in Russia* with the words: 'A fascinating book. It can be heartily recommended even to those who are tepid about dancing and drama and who neither like nor understand the East.'

Phogeys believe in keeping themselves to themselves, unlike the Americans, who believe in keeping other people to themselves. The English are said to be sexless; this is not true. It is simply that sex involves a group of two, and the English know that the ideal social group is one. In America, people will come up and talk to you anywhere, even in the toilet; there is no privacy, because who needs to be private? What are you hiding when you are?*

* Again, compare Sir Harold Nicolson, who puts the English view with regard to the Americans:
  'There is . . . the curious indifference to, or disregard of, what to us is one of the most precious of all human possessions, namely

Phogeys believe that communication is a very imperfect form of communication; or, to put it another way, that the function of speech is to conceal rather than to disclose ideas or emotions. There is a thing called PHATIC COMMUNION, which is communication at a sub-verbal level; animals have it. It is non-speech. It is the things that you say to someone when you are trying to say something else; phogeys have sub-verbal conversations with words. An excellent example is a phrase used by Americans called How Are You?, which is said to people when you don't want to know. It is fatal to reply to it by telling people how you are. I have seen, in Colorado, a woman who had just returned from having a ski accident, with one leg in plaster after a spiral break, and with bruises on her face, replying to this question. 'Fine, just fine,' she said, giving the correct response.† This is the key to English conversation. The English equivalent is the phrase, 'How do you do?' 'Do what?' unschooled Americans reply, falling into the trap (the whole purpose of the exchange is to separate the sheep from the goats, Our Lot from Their Lot); the correct response is, naturally, 'How do you do?' Phogeys live by such phatic communion; to do it properly shows that a chap must be half-way decent. Thus, in England, if you know things about your friends, you dis-cover that it is not because they have told you but because you have learned them by osmosis, gossip or inference. The

personal privacy. To them, with their proud belief in equality, with their rather ignorant affection for the pioneer spirit, privacy denotes something exclusive, patronizing, "un-folksey", and therefore meriting suspicion. Thus they leave their curtains undrawn at dusk, have no hedges separating their front gar-dens, and will converse amicably with strangers about private things. How can a European dare to discuss the manners of a people who seem to ignore, or to be unconscious of, what to him is civilization's most valued heritage?'

† Professor Howard Higman, a sociologist, suggests to us that, in the new American society, the phrase 'How are you?' should be amended to 'How's your group?'

English are non-communicative. Phatic communion is the exchange of meaningless words to work up a *gemütlich* atmosphere, so that afterwards it appears as if a conversation has actually taken place. I call this language *phogeycant*, that language of phogeys which performs all the functions of language except that of communicating meaning. There are certain key phrases which are the central commerce of phogeycant ('What things are coming to I don't know,' 'Don't rock the boat,' 'It's only human nature,' 'You'll live to regret it,' 'It can't be helped'), all of them having to do with the fact that things as they are, are best.

Phogey art is likewise meaningless. While detesting most serious art, because it creates discontent and *malaise* of the spirit, phogeys, working by Gresham's Law, have devised a kind of phogey art that is institutionalized, official, and ineradicable. Phogeys are generally not democrats, but in the field of culture they tend to be; they point out that only 50,000 people listen to the Third Programme, so why not get rid of it (of course the Third Programme is, on the other hand, itself phogeyfied). This type of phogey ranges from the Manchester alderman ('I don't know anything about art . . . etc.') to the phogey don for whom all art is by dead people. Note the Royal Academy, a phogey institution, and that Academician who attacked modern art, saying: 'I am right – I have the Lord Mayor on my side – and *all* the Aldermen – and all the City Companies.' When Picasso said, 'I have never heard of Annigoni,' Annigoni made a classical reply that must have endeared him to all phogey patrons of art. 'I have never heard of Picasso,' he said.

Phogey art is distinguished by its innocuousness; notice how phogeys tend to analyse a book or a play in terms of its ending ('It didn't have a proper ending'; 'It left things in the air a bit'). Art should leave no residuum. Phogey art also has GOOD CHARACTERS *and* FINE WRITING; in phogey magazine stories girls run across the moors, unkempt, but marry a doctor or the boss's son in the end. Phogeys dislike real art because it creates problems and leaves them unsolved. And phogeys do not like problems.

They dislike problems because they dislike people. They resent strangers, and consider always that they have enough friends, even if they have none. The Horatian tag – *Caelum non animum mutant qui trans mare currunt* (trans.: you can't get a decent cup of tea in France) – was surely written of the English. Seventy-seven per cent of the English, claimed some statistician a few years ago, have never been abroad. Of course things are changing. Many phogeys do go Abroad (to the phogey, Abroad is usually France) and the numbers increase each year. But now that everyone can do it, the best people don't need to any more; there is nothing conspicuous about it.

By and large, however, the New Continentalism, a rapidly growing phenomenon, is designed to provide all the advantages of being abroad without having to mix with all those foreigners. Espresso bars, motor scooters, Swedish furniture, Spanish music, Network Three Russian lessons, green raincoats – these are all part of the movement. How many of the mews cottage boys are having *lasagna* for dinner tonight? As a phogey young couple we observed (they wash their dog in Silvikrin, write away to Devonshire for spiced ginger advertised in the epicure columns of top papers) remarked, 'There are so many more things for the young these days, and they all seem to come from abroad.'

Older phogeys know this is nonsense, but prefer it to Americanization. Actually it is Americanization, for Americanization is just -ization. It is when you take things out of other societies and make them over to your use – quite absurd to the real phogey, who knows that English things are better, and distrusts the European Common Market for the proper reason that the English are neither European, nor Common. As an American friend remarked: 'What I admire about you Europeans is the way you've learned to live with other races . . .' 'This isn't Europe, this is England,' interrupted a phogey. 'Quite different.'

Phogeys do not like people. Above all they do not like women, and have difficulty in thinking of them as people at all. Women are the ones who get out and open the garage doors. Phogeys are far more interested in animals and property, and quite prefer them to people. In Budleigh Salterton there are more dogs than people and, as they will tell you (hanging on to their dogs, in case you are from the Russians) they prefer it that way. In the streets of England you will find ikons in the shape of large plaster dogs, before which people can worship by placing offerings of coin of the realm in a slot in the mouth provided for that purpose. 'What mischief have *you* been up to?' they say indulgently to their dogs. Alas, poor creatures, if they only knew what mischief was, and how to make it.

The division of the universe into two sexes has never struck the phogey as a useful one, and he has spent much of his history making artificial distinctions which are much more interesting. The result is the class system and the relative dullness of British women. Phogeys prefer their women not to look attractive; they feel it ostentatious and competitive. The classical English look, for women, is to appear as if you have just that moment got off a horse – tweeds and flat shoes and a twinset.

In so far as phogeys are concerned with people, which is as little as possible, they are concerned with their status or function. They protect the machinery of institutions with all the power at their disposal – measuring the size of carpets for Civil Service offices, having one lavatory for clerical staff and another for managers, insisting that only three standing passengers be allowed instead of five. It goes on at all levels, and as long as such persons survive, we can be sure that even in a classless society the necessary distinctions will be made, that it will remain, in short, England *their* England.

PART TWO

A
PORTPHOLIO
OF
PHOGEYS

The Hanging Judge

The Hanging Judge is a particularly English phenomenon. Took silk *c.* 1890, still calls taxis hansoms. England to him is divided into three classes: the decent, the working, and the criminal. This last, since they can no longer be transported, are to be kept in order by the whip and the rope. Psychology is a particularly repellent modern fad designed to undermine commonsense treatment of naturally evil men. Having bullied his wife to death (*c.* 1915) he lives alone, his sole reading being Famous Cases. Only really feels at home in this modern world under his black cap. Probably the most respected of venerable men and very imposing in his medieval garb.

Peace-time General

These are the men who start off Britain's wars and as we all know Britain starts off by losing, heavily. The peace-time general is then relegated to his desk, where he is quite happy in peace or war. Phogeydom is enshrined in the military; this is one of its main agencies, and of all the kinds of snobbery there is nothing like Services' snobbery. The phrase *Officer and Gentleman* was sadly chipped during the first world war, when so many officers were lost, because they persisted in going over the top unarmed, knowing that no decent jerry would shoot down an unarmed man who was obviously an officer, that they had to take officers from lower down the social scale. The rot set in then and it makes the peace-time general pretty mad, frankly. He can't understand how the Americans can get on without discipline, but then who wants to think about America anyway? He *looks* the soldier. He looks smart and big and dim and *English*. At his best on Dining-in nights when he plays all the games and mixes with the Subalterns, freely. He draws an enormous salary and, when he retires, aged about forty-five, an enormous pension. That big leather-bound book you see him carrying around with him is, of course, his Diary, and he has it in case he meets a Publisher who wants his memoirs (actually these memoirs are usually written by A.D.C.'s).

THE PROFESSIONAL GENTLEMAN

You may perhaps enjoy the good fortune to be standing by a professional gentleman when he is filling in a form, and against *Occupation* putting 'Gentleman'.

They are rarer than they were, but are still renowned for their manners. As the religious value morality, so the gentleman values Manners. 'It Makyth Man,' etc. Most of them are pretty poor nowadays, but manage an occasional shoot and do a bit of beagling. The Twelfth is for them what Christmas day is for the Workhouse, now. Generally speaking this is the figure that foreigners think of as typically English, and it was with a kind of English wit that we made one our Prime Minister. Old professional gentlemen are courteous and kind in the countryside (where bailiffs run their estates) while many are to be found orating peacefully in the House of Lords. To be in a position of real power, however, is so strange to them that they go about looking lost and murmuring: 'You've never had it so good.' Actually professional gentlemen have never had it so bad.

THE PHOGEY DIPLOMAT

He possesses three qualifications. He is a gentleman, he can speak French (in phogey-diplomat circles, at one time, speaking French equalled Gentlemen, but now all sorts of people can do it), and he is not bored with cocktail parties. Phogeyarch diplomats must have served their country and be, preferably, provincial lawyers. If attached to the Foreign Office, according to some reports, his morality must be of the modern kind (i.e. sin equals sickness, and vice versa).

To the diplomat nothing is actually *real* that doesn't go on in Embassies, Foreign Offices, Legations, Consulates, etc . . . The real world is recorded in his memoranda (*vide* Sir N. Henderson's reports on 1939 Berlin). However, since the life he leads is still maintained on an old-fashioned basis of protocol and entertaining, he is given over to the notion that people all still have servants and that England is still pretty much Edwardian really. As he only travels by car in specially selected areas he is rarely disabused. Actually he will only travel, in England, to places where there is *a local cheese*.

His way of writing has been subject to some ridicule. It is, it is true, vague to the point of meaninglessness and ignorant at times to the point of stupidity. This is all a FRONT, however, to dupe the Public into thinking that Diplomats don't know what they're doing. Reading his stuff the Public says: 'There's more in this than meets the eye'.

There is no room here for a glossary of phogey diplomat language, which concerns Stars, Doors and Crossroads. The new diplomats (Secret Covenants Openly Arrived At) are much perplexed by the influx of non-gentlemen into the field (in foreign countries, of course) and by the Dulles, or I-just-moved-the-chair-you-were-sitting-on approach.

Whatever we say, the Foreign Office will GO ON.

THE GENTLEMAN FARMER
Here is another RUS character, the Gentleman Farmer phogey. He is a snake-in-the-grass since he looks benevolent, but isn't.

His family once owned the Manor (which is now an experimental co-ed school) but he lives in the Lodge and cultivates fifty acres of the once vast estate. He can just afford to go to Hounds (never call them Dogs) and will, eventually, be Master if he can find someone to lift him up on his horse. He has a gammy leg from Passchendaele.

He is Coroner, on the local Borough Council and –

although not a member – dominates the Parish Council. He is against spending any money and is vitriolic in his condemnation of the Welfare State. His wife keeps Alsatians, which explains a lot. He has four girls, all with large behinds and boss eyes. Often he lives near Melton Mowbray, in the heart of the Chappie Dog Food country, a place where time stands still.

THE GENIAL ADMINISTRATOR

'We would like to do this for you but . . .' says the genial administrator, a very large class indeed. He is the Across-the-Office And Into-the-File-man. The bluffer ones have been in business, the more sedate in the Civil Service, the yellow and parched have worked abroad. All have diplomas and certificates of merit hung in their drawing rooms. This particular example is a Rosicrucian and therefore believes in Hidden Forces. He has a comfortable wife, THE house, THE car, THE lawn and now THE television. His life has been spent with paper. He remembers when they lost the file and when a fellow worker left a number off a Reference. His wife he came to as a virgin and he has had nothing to do with 'stenographers. He has no children, or perhaps one daughter who sings in the Bach choir, and keeps parakeets. He takes *Blackwood's* and makes periodic visits to the Vale of Evesham. He contributes to all the well-publicized charities.

THE DON

Most dons are phogeyarchs, but with the onset of television (they go, of course, for the meal beforehand, and not for the programme itself) the old adage 'Quiet Flows the Don' became out of date. Indeed, lately, Dons have been getting choleric before their time.

In the Humanities, however, Time, on the whole, is an irrelevant concept: All Souls is still the bastion of phogey-dom. What the Don does, in fact, counts less than what he STANDS FOR. He stands for CONTINUITY. A long line of Dons has preceded him, and a long line of hopeful, potential Dons sit at his feet, all wearing the appropriate duffel coats. Dondom is a state much desired by many men.

However, the Don must DO something. The most eminent publish book reviews. The least-known RESEARCH, and publish great works of scholarship which are eagerly bought by all potential Dons. They are known as Regular Fellows. Apart from these activities, dons walk through the Backs/down Addison Walk, looking donnish. They also savour sherry on the palate, though actually, one Don confessed, it all tasted like cold tea to him. They look behind the sofa, when they sit down, to see if C. P. Snow is there. To end the day, there is game for Dinner in the Great Hall and port in the Combination Room. In the latter place Dons show their utter abandon, discuss the physical measurements of M. Monroe. Then off to get on with the detective novel.

THE LADY ACADEMIC
I remember when we dug a splendid latrine at Brethermere back in '47. But Professor Hillesdon wouldn't let me near it. The suppressed woman who thinks she is consoled by the *long view* (i.e. that people have been making love for centuries without altering things much) but really isn't, *vide* her hysterics when her monograph is just noted by the T.L.S. among 'Books Received' and her ever-increasing study of ISIS (naughty doings in fourth-century Roman Villas). In fact she will probably end up as a volunteer guinea-pig in a new Carbon 14 experiment. To be saved from this, she must get into a TV programme where she can gaze on, and triumph academically over, Sir Mortimer Wheeler.

THE SOCIOLOGIST
The sociologist is really the poor man's psychologist. Although the individual doesn't get to know what's wrong

with *him* (unless he is SELECTED as being *typical*,* for a pilot survey) he gets to know what's wrong with *society*. For it is social *trends* and *manifestations* that the Sociologist is interested in. As he says, social studies doesn't deal with people really; it's a science. And how he wishes that it were (sometimes he secretly spells it with a 'p' – 'psociology' – to make it sound more scientific).

However the sociologist must be able to get on with people, be able to write bad English and cultivate Humility. He should also know how to draw a confusing graph or two.

But, as he will tell you, it is People, ultimately, who do count. He has a look ORDINARY, perhaps even artisanish, since he has to measure skirting boards and examine furniture, see if walls are papered or painted, visit private privies, examine babies' toenails – DO ANYTHING, in fact, which tells him HOW PEOPLE ARE LIVING. Then he tells us how people ought to live.

He works by observation. He observes, for instance, that in a big city you get your feet trodden on more often than in a small town. What is the actual incidence of feet-treading (he takes a sample)? What is its relationship to class? Are feet-treaders predominantly socially mobile? Is there any correlation between feet-treading and increase in crime? What is the history of feet-treading? Is it recorded before the industrial revolution? Is it a specifically urban phenomenon? Is there any implicit class-hostility? What social abrasions does it conceal? Is it alleviated by town planning. . . ?

He is often a genial chap, full of bonhomie, as all those people are who discover yet another easy ride. To be a sociologist, the only qualification is to be a person.

THE PHOGEY AUTHOR
Though rarely seen in England, except as a guest of honour at Foyle's Literary Luncheons where he is acclaimed 'Mas-

---

* To be TYPICAL, you have to live near a sociologist.

ter of the Short Story', he is more English than most of us. By living abroad, or deep in the country, he holds on to the Old England, when there really was a single line extending from Windsor to Wormwood Scrubs of all individuals all justly and precisely graded. He has always had a private income and his novels sell well among the cultured u.m.c. He lived on the Left Bank (when the Left Bank was the Left Bank), an intimate friend of minor Impressionists, and he may even have met Proust, or André Gide. When you meet him in Paris he insists on talking French and even in pretending that he isn't English. At any rate he is highly sympathetic to French culture, knows Saint-Beuve backwards, and when he was young used to tour down the Dordogne. Has developed a taste for sherries. No interviews. Latest work a highly garbled account of the TEN BEST POEMS of the TEN BEST POETS, written with one eye on United States sales, because there they like to know what is best. He read *Lucky Jim* and remarked that if this were what things were coming to, he was glad he hadn't lived to see it. The point of this comment was that writers are traditionally upper middle; everyone knows that, and their job, as 'civilized beings', is to give delight, not go on about what they *think*. Gentlefolk (i.e. the core of the British reading public) don't want that; one deduces from this a new reading public.

PRACTICAL SANDS
This can be called the PRACTICAL SANDS type; found cluttering up the arts at all its points. If in the theatre, knew Granville Barker and carried GBS's bag once on Nuneaton Station; he also once played the steward in *St Joan*. In the literary world, knew Chesterton, whence comes his paradoxical wit, and was on *The London Mercury* under J. C. Dislikes criticism and prefers book reviews, which he does for the *Illustrated London News* or similar, persuading readers not to buy young authors. Wrote a bit himself, and published a book of Travel Essays in 1912. Essentially the gentleman amateur, he deplores the growing professional-

ism of the young. If a very practical sands type, he probably spent some time on the *Manchester Guardian* under Scott, doing travel and the cricket, or on the *Evening Standard* under Beaverbrook. Likes port and cultivates eccentricities such as the public wearing of slippers. Hopes one day to be asked by the B.B.C. to do 'My Great Contemporaries'.

Wonders how young men in *vie des lettres* can manage, without a valet, to find time. Dressing takes so long by oneself. Condemns the modern novel for, of course, *nostalgie de la boue*. The artist must, he complains, *constater*.

THE BENSON AGE PHOGEY*

Why, in my day we had the Young GBS, Wells, Bennett, Chesterton, Belloc and that lad Rupert Brooke – what splendid chaps they were! Oscar had only just passed out of the picture, the scallywag, but we had Max, ah, the incomparable Max! What days they were. Hansoms, you know, and gallantly dressed men who had manners, and women who looked really *feminine*, one doesn't see gels like that nowadays. We had Galsworthy, too: I got him to sign my copy of his great book *The Forsyte Saga*, I'm leaving you that in my will. We shan't ever see their like again – the Music Hall, Tommies, Kitchener, Pack Up Your Troubles in Your Old Kit Bag – those were bags, you know, that soldiers carried, there were a lot of them about then. Lovely days. Now what have you got? D. H. Lawrence† and his kidney, and Winston Churchill saying we ought to get out of India. Pah! And the wireless. I used to ask God to spare me a few more years but I'm hanged if I want to live any longer. No spirit now, no guts, no life. Hah, you don't know, me boy, you just don't know . . .

* Benson Age: so called in memory of Frank Benson, who acted Shakespeare in provincial towns *c.* 1910. He was a bad, but gifted, actor.
† Non-literary people think DHL is still pouring out pornography.

He is not against anything in the world, except Britain and the *Daily Express*. He is, in a nutshell, the representative of the French way of life, abroad. He is a scholar and therefore *gentle*. His work, being cultural, is universally despised. Actually he goes to a great deal of trouble to collect together anti-British magazines (like the *New Statesman*) in his reading room and to hold meetings to tell the Afro-Asians he wouldn't live in Britain at any price, and isn't this rather a nice little wine.

He runs the Film Society, showing French films, and the Play-reading Group, reading French plays. He may be expert at Yoga/Buddhist Folk Initiations. All in all, he leads a pleasant life as an outpost of civilization and manages to get through Proust every half year. He thinks the Wolfenden Report was the best thing to come out of England for many a long year.

He is much better than the *Daily Express* says he is.

CITY MAN

Vespas are all right now, you know – even with a bowler hat.

Only young yet, he is as inveterate a phogeyarch as the ancientest. 'It's a pity society apportions its praises and blames as it does, but what can one do about it?' he asks in liberal surroundings, for there are so many of these nowadays. 'After all,' says his wife, 'there's always some injustice, isn't there?'

He is adjusted to things as they are. As he says if there's any class system in England now, it's all in the minds of the lower classes. He is not born but trained. Public school (or sub-public school) has taught him the accent; Cambridge taught him the right end to punt from and how life has its idylls ('I prefer holding your hand the *other* way'). Girls wear bright summer dresses, carry parasols; underneath, however, a wool vest. At Grantchester, by God, there *is* honey still for tea. Looks, like Rupert Brooke, for a hundred girls to kiss (in a good, clean English way, of course) and a hundred songs to sing (but of course there's only one song to sing, the song about swinging together). This led to a smart Guards Regiment which led to the City. He is now one of the Edward boys (i.e. the type the *Daily Mirror* used to picture with the caption: Too Many Mothers Want Their Sons To Look Like This). What was so galling was that chaps like Finch-Carr (our sample) got on to the New Edwardianism first. Their clothes were ever so slightly Edwardian; the trend started in the best (i.e. Guards) regiments and spread through the city (Stock Exchange/Insurance/Banking) to the East End. The shame of it: as Finch-Carr told us, 'Decent people daren't appear in fancy waistcoats any more.'

He is absolutely typed, a pure protocol boy from the word go. The accent, the subjects of conversation, the car, the newspaper – all can be remorselessly ticked on the list as soon as this figure is seen. He waits for his bus, a Top Person.

THE TOWNSMAN PHOGEY

An utter townsman who imagines, because he has read W. H. Davies and 'Grantchester', that his roots are in the country, and he only needs his belly close to the earth to find his real self. He visits friends who have a Quaint Olde Worlde Cottage (leaking thatch, earth-pit privy, well-water) and who do healthy work (milking cows with chapped teats at four a.m., hoeing sugar-beet all day, etc.) and have healthy entertainment (the Pub), and believes that they have SOUND VALUES. He goes into his friend's garden: 'Oh, how lucky you are having all these lovely vegetables FREE!' He asks about his rent – five shillings. 'Oh, how lucky you are! How much milk and firewood does he give you? – As much as you can cart away! Oh, how lucky you are. I really think I must come and live in the country.'

This explains why, throughout history, men have tended to congregate in the country, neglecting the towns.

We all of us know this kind of Stunt Man, who was interested in Eskimos and Red Indians from his earliest youth and at school smoked a pipe in the latrine when everyone else was thinking in terms of cigarettes. If he ever had a car it was called The Little Bug or The Flying Devil and probably even had an umbrella stand. Often he belonged in the IMITATION UNDERGRADUATE category. These people wear scarves and blazers with badges and are to be found singing. 'Oh, Sir Jasper' in espresso bars. Usually they turn out to be bank clerks. They are frequently about to sail round the world in a forty-foot yacht, which they don't yet quite have. They joined the Raff and came to their own fighting the Battle of Britain, which was just their sort of show.

Now round the camp fire Gerald (Arm Me Audacity) Perkins will, on occasion, tell of Tough Moments when the Sherpa tied a Granny (precipitous beginning, what?) or when Reg, finding Americans *stationed* at the South Pole, broke down and cried. You have, however, to get from hints why he — and others — do these feats of dare-devilry. Mockers say they do it to get away from their wives. Others say they do it for the Newspapers. Whatever the reason, Gerald and his pals set a fine example to Outward Bound, and while we have men like them pot-holing away all over we shan't go far wrong. Shall we?

THE GOOD SPORT
'Mens sana, corpore sano,' said the headmaster to this young phogey, and he formed the mistaken impression that he *had to choose*, not being bright at Latin anyway. So he became a *corpore sano* phogey. He is found in County places – in country pubs with town conveniences, at points to point, and at the boathouse or the rugby club social. He wears a flat cap (cut, of course, from *one* piece of cloth, and therefore non-workman) and a blazer. He has, in this order, a sports car ('the old crock'), a dog ('the old pal'), a wife

('the old gel'). He is full of exploits stories – how the boys threw the Leander stroke into the Thames at Henley last year, and he drowned; how they gatecrashed the rugby club dance ('climbed in through the window of the bog; found someone was pulling my feet; said, don't be a fool, man, don't pull, push; found it was a bobby'), how they 'captured' beer mugs from a public house ('Not us, officer, I said, it must have been someone else, and he was just going to let us go when Bill, silly chump, opens the door and the whole lot went rolling out and smashed right at the bobby's feet').

Now he is getting, as he puts it, a bit long in the tooth, and things aren't so good. He has said all his life that sport's the thing, swing, swing together and all that tosh, let's not get serious or we might go off the rails. He rows stroke still, but more often coaches; he can still be seen on sunny days oiling his cricket bat. But now he bats in the tail, and still, trying to be a sport about it, he accosts the skip before the match: 'Where am I in the batting order this week, skip? Down in the tail? Still, you're the skip. Consistently bad play I could understand it, but bad luck ... Still, it's the game that counts. It's just that Bracken, your predecessor, used to give me opening knock. Oh, I'm not blaming you, I know I was a bit younger. Still, he always said there was no one like me for putting off their fast bowling. Well, I know Wilson gets good scores, I'd be the last to deny it, but you can't call it good stroke plan. Off-drive? More of a push, I'd call it . . .'

EIGHTY-YEAR-OLD ATHLETE

Anyone who thinks the English are not resilient should go down to the beach and take a look at the eighty-year-old athlete. He is down there at six every morning, does the crawl out to the harbour wall and back, and returns scarcely breathing hard. Wheat germ has done this for him, that and looking after himself. The eighty-year-old athlete is often liberal-minded and has taught W.E.A. classes on The Rise of Capitalism. Nudism attracted him for a spell, though he didn't like being shut in; and vegetarianism also exerted its spell, though he found it difficult when you thought that eggs were potential hens and shoes were made from cows, and even sofas were stuffed with horsehair. Secretly, however, what interested him about both these disciplines was that they seemed to keep you healthy.

His wife is usually an eighty-year-old athlete as well, and sits on the beach holding his jock strap until he gets back from the swim, wearing slacks that were knitted by the blind in 1938 ready for the war in Europe.

The Right Wife

Most English women, luckily for them, come into this category. Before they marry they say: 'John, dear, I've told you before, you *mustn't* kiss me in the street,' and afterward they say: 'Behave yourself, dear, there's a time and place for everything.'

Being in love with English women is a pretty hard cross for men to bear; they say, 'John, I really shall have to do something about you; I'm beginning to notice a few faults.' However, they are sensible, provident, and cook a good meal, and as any Englishman will tell you, they make the best wives in the world.

Mostly they bear one or two children ('Catch me going through that again'); when the girls reach puberty they are locked in or, alternatively, out (see any advice column in any women's paper for letters on this subject). To their boys they say: 'Madam Right will come along one day; till then, be a good boy.' Looking for an explanation of the transmission of this congenital sexlessness, one instinctively blames the weather. However, looking deeper, one sees the ghastly after-effects of Mother-Schooling which emphasizes the need for the RIGHT HUSBAND/WIFE but never explains what he/she is for. Nor does it explain the place of FEELINGS. Feeling feelings is an adolescent phenomenon that wears off.

PREDOMINANTLY EQUESTRIAN

*And then Helen fell at the water-jump and bust her breeches
– talk about laugh – saw arse and all.*

In the ditch lies the Predominantly Equestrian Phogey.
Broad-shouldered, husky and broad-bottomed, the Horsey/
Doggy woman loves all Male Animals, but not all human
males.

She has an interesting history. When she was young it was
observed that she looked dreadful off a horse. Since then she
has been off one rarely, and even then she plays the 'cello,
because she also looks dreadful off a 'cello. She has a
high-pitched whinny and is full of jokes about riding side-
saddle. Swears, drinks, wears corduroy trousers (with flies)
and busty aertex shirts. Frequently cultivates moustache.
Absolute political reactionary, believing FORCE can solve all
problems. She spends most of her terra firma time in the
stables, because work is always piling up there.

THE CHARLUS PHOGEY

Oh! I'm so pleased you think my glasses suit me! And, as I
was saying, *what is* the *use* of scholarship if one can't
interest the young in it? I'm writing the most terribly
interesting book.

As I was saying, the English are such puritans. Look at
poor Oscar. You can bet your life that old Club-ridden
judge had seen a thing or two in his time . . . But perhaps
I'm embarrassing you? No?

Yes, I will, please. Mine's a Gin and Orange.

As I was saying when you were getting the drinks (how
nice your haircut looks from behind), I'm writing a book on
Queen Elizabeth. Oh, she was a proper old tomcat, wasn't
she? Do you know what a Bishop said when she died? 'The
King is dead. Long live the Queen.' That was in reference to
that little idiosyncrasy of dear Jamie One. We all have our
little failings, don't we? Don't you think it's stuffy in here?
Why not come back and play my new tape recorder –

awfully 'spensive but I got the whole of that Third Programme Madrigal Session . . .

THE RETIRED SCHOOLMASTER

He loves tea and whist drives and is a great gossiper. He does a bit of gardening but doesn't read much now because his eyesight is failing. He is usually found in quaint cottages in quaint villages. His cultured voice and odd Latin tags lead the yokels to feel that he is a gentleman. He sends his help to get his pension. He wears herring-bone suits – 'Takes me back to my registers, y'know.'

THE FATHER OF THE FLOCK PHOGEY

When a curate (c. 1925) he was all things to all men – it was all right, then, to be a communist or, alternatively, an atheist. In his declining years he finds himself nothing to no men. Long ago he commuted his tithes and wrote a History of the Church. His faithful flock are now so few and have been so faithful that he no longer makes the effort to read his printed sermons of a Sunday. Instead he makes them feel cosy by asking rhetorically: Why don't people come to church? and hinting strongly that those who don't will be consigned to Hell Fire. At least they, however, will be warm; it is a big church and his flock are not. If his few are spinsters he adds, quite often, a bit on the virtue of virginity and the sins of concupiscence. He has never heard of the Dead Sea Scrolls, in fact he leans toward being HIGH: he may upset his Sexton/Verger by erecting an Altar to Mary, or Joan of Arc. In his last years he may even use incense, which, he explains, helps to keep the bats away. The Bishop may complain that he is *out of touch*; in which case he has only to ask the Bishop his advice on how to get in touch.

He has a frail wife, who reads the *Telegraph*. He is an ardent Bibliophile, being particularly interested in Old Books with Leather Bindings.

This is a particularly pernicious kind of phogey, because his function is to bring the phogeys to the phogeys, on television, on radio, on the cinema screen and in the pages of the press. 'I'm getting tired of foreigners coming over here and telling us how to run things,' they say, and the phogeys say to one another: 'Isn't that just what I've been saying?'

Some appear with bear-like irritations in the popular press under fancy pseudonyms, some classical and thought out when he was up at Cambridge (ATTILA THE HUN, CYCLOPS) and some matey (EVADNE POOP, JOHN FLEET). One of his social functions is to instigate the persecution of any novel concerned with serious human relationships in a serious manner. He hasn't much time for sensitives and the uncommon man, because they don't buy the things in the adverts. Stepping out of the pattern is *un-British* and what he is more than anything is the BRITISH MORALIST. He is Senator McCarthy in a good clean sort of way. He appeals to different sections of public taste, according to his readership, but whoever he appeals to, he really *appeals*. He gives people so much of what they want that they soon actually begin to want it. He is, of course, essentially uncritical, while appearing to be critical to the highest degree.

Then there is the PATIENCE WEAK television personality, whose off-the-cuff chatter is Socratic wisdom to millions. He is tied to phogeydom, because he has constantly to invent resentments or else people complain he is slipping. He is the great figure of our age, THE FALSE AUTHORITY.* Though he grouses, everyone knows he has a heart of gold, especially lady viewers who fall in love with him (loving at second-hand, like living at second-hand, is one of the sad comedies of our age).

---

* FALSE AUTHORITY is based on the universal premise that anyone who succeeds in one field is qualified to discourse on all others. Thus skill at making motor-cars entitles Henry Ford to say, 'History is bunk' – and the thing is, PEOPLE LISTEN.

The obverse of the PATIENCE WEAK phogey is the PATIENCE STRONG phogey, who purveys phogey *gemütlich* (Th'art the finest old man of 140 Ah've ever met!) instead of phogey irritability. He is for the phogeysite what the other is for the phogeyarch, his public spokesman. He brings home, for them, the things that are LASTINGLY TRUE — that mums are the backbone of the race, that everyone's had an interesting life and lots of embarrassing experiences, that everyone deserves something for nothing, that old folk are champion, that *everyone can sing.*

Both are sad figures, from their own point of view because in a better world they would not have to do this, and from ours, because they do.

THE OLD CHINA HAND
Note the eyes. This is a practical example of the thesis that if you are far-sighted enough you can bargain away your YOUTH for a comfortable old age. He is actually the man who is always writing to the editor complaining how hard inflation is on those with FIXED incomes. He decided early on that since he was a Bachelor and had no Friends he would have to provide for his Old Age. This he did through Insurance Policies/investing his money in the Suez Canal/going to China. He is now, he will tell you, *laughing.* However he is also crying (because of inflation). Sometimes he has a quirk of regret for those lost sixty years. He is a vegetarian, non-smoker and non-drinker. His hero is Lord Cherwell. On his death his fortune and assets will go to the State, and be spent on Family Allowances.

THE YOUTH LEADER
The important thing to keep in mind is the difference between the phogeyarch and the phogeysite, for this is the crux of the phogey problem. Without the one there could not be the other. The phogeyarch ensures the continuance of phogeydom, by seeing that none but the cream of the phogeysites succeed him. He says, soon be time to give the

younger fellars a chance; but he is old, old before he does, and by younger fellows he means people of fifty or more. Much stress is placed on tradition; phogeys *carefully* relinquish their places. There is one infallible way to identify the phogeyarch; he is always called *Sir* by American servicemen. But how to identify the phogeysite? Look, first, for his ambition to rise, and look for his fear of being found out. Even if he has nothing to hide he may be found out. His great virtue is his steadfastness, for which he pays hardly. His respect – for law, order, institutions, keeping off the grass – is extraordinary and infinitely exploitable, as the Inland Revenue and the Government ('I wouldn't be so stupid as to use a car in London' – *Minister of Transport*) have found out. He talks in phogeycant. 'Everything in the garden's lovely,' he says; or 'Don't rock the boat,' or 'It's one thing after another, isn't it?' or 'It's a small world.'

The phogey nearly always achieves a position of some power, and no position is more coveted than that of YOUTH LEADER. He sometimes looks deceptively young. He is a dedicated man, devoted to Youth and the cause of *saving youth from themselves*. He is usually single, and plays a sort of tennis. His method of locomotion (his phrase) is a bicycle. He knows the Peak District backwards and makes a bi-annual tour of the Lakes. He may on occasion lead a GROUP to Edinburgh to the festival, or adventure abroad, even, to the Healthy (i.e. Scandinavian but not Sweden) countries.

His catch line is 'Now boys and girls . . .' He really believes that if he goes on teaching all these healthy things the young will, one day, break out into *spontaneous morris dancing*. Then he would be vindicated. He is trusted by all phogey parents to keep, on mixed expeditions, the boys from straying among the girls (or vice versa), or even spotting that girls are different and looser-fitting. He always does encourage CLEANLINESS and DECENCY. Into the same category fall Scoutmasters and Choirmasters. The Youth Leader is often an Executive Civil Servant.

The Social Creep

Without the social creep, phogeyarchs couldn't exist. He is the man who keeps the upper class upper (and the phogeys, phogeys) because by carefully calculated social clumsiness (non-U language, peas on knife, etc.) and generalized social crawling ('Lovely flowers, your ladyship,' etc.) he convinces phogeyarchs that any doubts that they might have in the Welfare State of their continued usefulness are unfounded. He is well-represented in B.B.C. seventeenth-century plays by the Innkeeper type and his modern embodiment is the commentator with the HALLOWED voice who does the coronations for television.

He has worked for 'Gentry' all his life, and kow-towing becomes him. He has a permanent stoop in his back and his eyes are always uplifted. He is getting bald now, and so has a false forelock to touch. He is now probably looking after a gentleman's horses, or gardens, or pheasants. With him as gamekeeper, Sir Clifford Chatterley would have had no worry. Wherever he is, he reflects THEM, although, he will tell you, he is careful to keep his place. Also says that 'Gentlemen-born' have NO SIDE. He wears the Squire's old clothes. He is usually ruddy and fat. It is well to emphasize the fact that when the CREEP dies out, so will THE MASTER.

The Whoops! What Gear Am I In Phogey

'I'm not paying a man seven or eight pounds a week for a boiling of kidney beans,' you can hear her saying forthrightly in the village. In plays, she is always seen in verandah pieces, a cross between Margaret Rutherford and Edith Evans. Sometimes she is a stout old body, sometimes frail and thin, sometimes she is a spinster who talks to her bird and sometimes she has a husband and dashes in and out of the house saying, 'Get your own tea, dear, will you?' to him, poor devil, who doesn't even know what W.V.S. stands for.

She is usually to be found in the garden, with her gardening gloves on, snipping off the dead roses and saying, 'Have you got the fly too, dear?' She makes plum jam and smashes the stones to get out the goodness. She works for women's organizations and is always arranging talks with titles like 'Whither China?' or even 'China – Whither?' The talks are usually given by retired admirals. Sometimes she comes out with a surprising word: 'Bloody hot today, eh, admiral?' She sometimes fits corsets for the village and embarrasses young girls by staying in the booth too long and looking too closely. She is, in fact, highly skittish and she has a little car, which she drives on either side of the road indiscriminately. It's difficult to know whether it's worse to drive with her or be telephoned to go out and fetch her when she's broken down (she is, of course, usually just out of petrol). 'What's this knob my handbag's hanging on?' she asks. 'Whoops! That was a near thing. Got bumped up the behind the other day. What gear am I in? You know, dear, I like having the gear-lever down on the floor – stops the men getting at your legs. Whoops! Whoops! Did anything fall?'

She really misses the Edwardian wilderness, when men kissed her in the conservatory and she had, as she tells people, a bloody great orchid stuck down between her . . . in her bosom.

THE DISEASE PHOGEY OR CORONARY THROMBOSOID
A ruddy, healthful soul who always has to say: 'My looks don't pity me.' England is FULL of them, all drawing pensions and National Assistance.

Got lazyitis around forty-five and read a Medical Book which said that it wasn't a genuine complaint; so he had to look for one. Financial Cramp wasn't, either. Since he was suffering from both these and no one would listen, he asked a friend who had a Heart how he got it. Friend advised mental strain as a short cut to Coronary Thrombosis (this is *the* thing to have had, of course, in England). Phogey then read the *Encyclopaedia Britannica* through in a week, concocted traumas out of adolescent experiences he hadn't thought about for years and listened to the B.B.C. Third Programme. Stricken within a week. Doctor advised complete rest and close attention and definitely no worries. Now recovered, he faces another thirty years of utter relaxation. Says people without a Heart don't appreciate what people who have a Heart feel like. Our advice in dealing with this is: Have a Heart.

SUNDAY SCHOOL TEACHER
And there He was – the Lord standing in the corner of the cornfield.
A Spinster, who has existed for forty years on Brewery shares left by her father, she knits and lets cats sleep on the bed. Probably has done a bit of non-certified teaching in her time; hence her interest in Sunday School, where she can retail her mystic experiences. Once genuinely intent and learned, she is now frail and cranky, loneliness and desolateness have upset her basic and formerly common-sensical balance. A sad figure.

An associated figure is the WOMEN'S INSTITUTE LECTURER ('Now we have the plums nicely washed and the water nicely boiling – will Mrs Smith tell us what we do with the nicely clean bottles?') who gives lectures on Dusting for Health and Household Management. Sometimes on these Institute occasions, games (hunt the thimble) or cards (whist) are resorted to. A real *gemütlichkeit* pervades such gossiping groups and they are duly reported in the local papers.

THE 'ARD, 'ARD PHOGEY
Usually a Yorkshireman, and 'ard, 'ard. Entirely self-made, and therefore built of sturdy stuff, and self-educated (apart from Night Classes) he is a Human Dynamo. When there's trouble up at th'mill, he is why.

He remembers his father with whom he built their first *fac*tory, brick by bloody brick, and put up their first *no*tice outside, which *pro*claimed HARDCASTLE AND SON. Since then, things have got worse. His father died, for a start, and they 'ad to 'ave a funeral at the public expense. Then he (the son) married, a homely lass, and that was before he 'ad the BIG HOUSE in which he could incarcerate the woman. It was a 'ard slog. She scrubbed th'flowers (i.e. floors) and took i'th' washin' from th'nobs who could afford to pee (pay, of course). She still does.

One thing he gained, however, was RESPECT. No Union Chaps on his place. What he says, goes. He has also gained BRASS. The factory prospered. Now there are twenty-five factories with notices outside that say HARDCASTLE.

For relaxation this phogey reads The *Financial Times* and the *Yorkshire News*, he 'as controlling interest in the latter because he 'as views, and wants them known. As he says, what's happiness, you can't buy money with it. But he does have principles, and as he declares forthrightly, there's nowt like a chap that sticks by his principles, even if you have to pay a bit more for him.

His only regret is that he didn't write that book on How to Achieve Success before Lord Beaverbrook.

THE GHOUL
Cor, then they laid 'im out – dreadful end 'e 'ad – then they couldn't get his eyes ter close. I says, 'e's not as bad as Mrs Pritchett, cor we 'ad a time with 'er, kept passing water involuntary like right up to the finish . . .
This is a medieval figure, always either laying out or laying in. She is a midwife and her conversation centres around disease and death. She wears black always and has a running nose, and is enjoyable in small doses.

In virtue of her position, she feels in close touch with the medical profession and is a social climber. She loves to speak of the ladies, real ladies, she had nursed and how good they were at the end, and how she was the best layer out in Newmarket before the war.

THE GOSSIP
What they do is their business but . . .
All phogeys are curious but find it hard to admit, because

phogeys nominally keep themselves to themselves. The l.c. phogey wanting to look out of the window shakes a duster; the middle-class phogey peers from behind lace curtains; while the u.c. phogey just damn well looks.

The gossip is possibly too old to peer, but entertains her friends who give her the griff on all that is happening, has happened, will happen. If an occasional peerer, she has grist enough to provoke the mills of all the gossips in the neighbourhood. While wholeheartedly inquisitive, her comments often have no moral bias; they are just information. Most old-phogey women are kept alive for their last ten years by interesting themselves in other people's business. They wear mittens and ankle-coverings and knitted cardigans; they drink tea incessantly and have cats.

In England, lover's lanes are usually labelled. This is not for the benefit of lovers, but for those who go there to watch.

Notice, too, the function of THE HEDGE. It is to talk to neighbours over.

THE DELICATE DRUNK

There is little time to go into gentility, but all delicate drunks are genteel. To them Gin and Orange, or Stout, is the key to Salvation. They have either married young to an old phogey, and so have plenty of cash; or they now keep a boarding house; or have lost their loved one (*really* loved one) and have fifteen children.

A strange variant of them is the MADAM ('As I always says, we're only here once and the Lord don't mind us having a bit of fun'), who loves men and likes to help them along, in all sorts of ways.

If all phogeys were like these, one wouldn't be too inclined to grumble.

THE T.U. PHOGEY

Usually north-country, with bags of PUSH and a carefully emphasized dialect, he found his voice early on and his mates, accepting the fact that they had discovered a spokesman, passed the cap round and sent him to night school. He still has the cap and wears it on television. Here he read Marx and Hobson and G. D. H. Cole, perhaps even a bit of Shaw and the Hammonds. Disgusted with the plight of the working classes, which he now began to notice, he readily accepted paid Secretaryship of a Local Union. Fortune was made when he got into a photograph with E. Bevin as latter was leaving No. 10, all set to abandon the General Strike.

He is not a Lord, nor even a Labour MP, but has a comfortable life and still wants to see all other working men lead comfortable lives. He, however, has come to see that there are two sides to every question and, while losing none of his sincerity, his proposals are noticeably VAGUER though not less VITRIOLIC. He still sees his mates on annual outings, and even remembers some of their Christian names. His wife has a help and has recently bought an electric washing machine with the interest from his shares.

THE RETIRED RAILWAYMAN
This retired Methodist railwayman is taken as representative of a large group of phogeys. He is the anti-pleasure Puritan. He lost his wife in childbirth, his twins from diphtheria and his eldest daughter from rabies; his father died of drink and drank away what little he'd got saved. He is therefore against pets, sex, disease, smoking and Demon Drink. He hangs up notices in Public Houses saying: NO DANCING, NO SINGING, and even NO LAUGHING. He forbids Sunday Cinema. Unfortunately from his point of view he tends to have little influence (except in Wales) over youth since his lectures at Youth Fellowship meetings are sparsely attended. They are about Evil. He is a Conservative, and reads the *Daily Mail*. Some members of this group are known to take walks in parks at night and some – even the most respectable – have been known to become suddenly disgraced.

The pity about him is, he turns people against morality, which is a BAD THING.

The Harridan is usually found behind the counters of Railway Station buffets or on Corporation buses, and what distinguishes her is that, unlike the rest of us, she has not got all day. 'My God,' she says, leaning affectedly on an arm, if you are slow at choosing between ham or cheese sandwiches, 'I've not got all day, you know.'

She is one of the reasons why coming back to England is such an ordeal, and why everything seems so grim and grey when you get here. She is known as an 'ard woman and treats her customers as if they were purposely stupid or nasty or both. She always has *special* customers with whom she is pally ('Sugar, Fred?') and whom she, in fact, treats with exaggerated respect, as if to emphasize how much she loathes Humanity in general. She has never heard of the Dignity of Labour. Such women (if on buses) sometimes have 'ard shiny slacks in which they encase their 'ard shiny thighs.

The male counterpart of the Henna-haired Harridan is the It-Can't-Be-Helped-Can-It Clerk, to be found in railway booking offices, post offices and on buses. For him the bus does not turn a wheel before the last three on get off, driving licences are not issued in working hours, and regulations never permit. This Clerk has one notable physical characteristic; he only has two hands, you know.

THE MAKE DO AND MEND OR RAINY DAY MAN

Do-it-yourself was started with this figure in mind, but, of course he always did. Finds things rather easy now. He has a cold appearance, due to his nicely balanced diet, and short hair. He is found only at work. He smokes home-made cigarettes and never drinks, because people who drink come home and are sick on the carpet. Perhaps he has a TV set, but only because it is respectable. If there is an institute in the village, or a library in the town, he goes down occasionally to read the *Encyclopaedia Britannica*. He has a scrawny wife who dresses from Marks and Spencers and probably two haggard children.

He attends jumble sales and is proficient at whist. Many of these persons are craftsmen. Invariably they have large gardens (or THE allotment) of which they are inordinately proud and which produce produce. If he has a sport, the Rainy Day man is an angler, for angling is cheap and quiet and thoughtful. Of course he eats all the fish he catches. He keeps hens and every so often he sits in the henhouse all night with a hammer, without moving, until a rat puts in an inquisitive nose. Then . . . *bang*!

THE NOW LET'S DO SOMETHING SIGNIFICANT OR WORK-ING-CLASS INTELLECTUAL PHOGEY

Probably a journalist, but may work in a shoe-shop or be a solicitor's clerk. Was introduced to a GROUP when he was fifteen and has since then been group-minded. Has acted in Greek tragedy (sheets, etc.) and is adept on the recorder, on which he plays Benjamin Britten-y tunes, beginning 'Heigh-ho'. Prefers to play outside, if possible. When the group goes out, as a Group, they visit places of Historical Interest, and the Royal Festival Hall; when they stay in, they do play-readings. They talk about people DESTROYING one another with love, and their characters are open books to one another, because they talk about them so often. Every morning they write down their dreams for the GROUP to hear in the evening. They keep a diary, and the entries often begin: 'The agony continues – unabated' or 'I must do something violent or go crazy'. They reflect on *die Grabheit des Pöbels*, (i.e. the coarseness of the rabble). Usually this phogey is called Fred (all the members of the group are known by their Christian names). Fred is usually an under-cover Toc H man. The Group only drinks coffee and when it talks, it usually talks RELIGION and BEAUTY and DEATH, which subjects are, as Fred says, what life is ABOUT.

THE ÉMIGRÉ

Apart from the fact that he frequents the British Museum Reading Room (which is entirely given over to Mittel-Europeans and Americans), the émigré is more English than the English – in fact, he often *is* English, and affects to be like that. He carries his food about in a paper bag and eats it in a teashop, throwing scraps to the mice as he does so. He is prodigiously knowledgeable, in the German tradition of scholarship, and the word MYTH features much in his conversation. 'Ahha,' he cries, shaking a roguish finger, 'You English, you are the most liberal nation in ze world. You lent Karl Marx the British Museum to write *Das Kapital*. Now you let me write my book. This is why Khrushchev says, We shall bury you. But you vill still be here ven de state has disappeared.'

His book is an appeal to the English working classes to slaughter their intellectuals before it is too late. He is very sincere and enriches English society by coming. The truth is, of course, that all intellectual advances in England over the last fifty years seem to have been made by foreign expatriates. He may look new here, but actually he knew Gissing and watched Marx's hat in the reading room while Marx went to the lavatory.

THE IRREDENTIST

One of the most unfortunate things that ever happened in this isle, in the view of the irredentist, was the conjunction of all its races into a single unit. All irredentists want to break things down. They want Home Rule for Scotland or Ireland or Penge. Irredentists imagine that their part of the world has a unique and distinctive culture and can survive independently as a nation. The Scotch Irredentist (never call Scots Scotch unless you feel you can get away with it) is kilted or trewed, with bagpipes bursting and reciting Robbie Burns, and he tosses bombs into Elizabeth II letterboxes to prove that the Scots are civilized. All of them play the bagpipes, well or badly (with the bagpipes of course one simply can't tell). There are a lot more things to say about the Scotch but I have na the patience.

The Welsh irredentist is a Celt, a man of romance, imagination and WORDS. Especially words, spoken or sung. Especially sung. All Welshmen sing, whether they can or not. There is, however, much to be said for this, as is clear if one compares them with Irish irredentists, who ought to be got into male voice choirs as quickly as possible.

PART THREE

HOW TO HAVE CLASS IN A CLASSLESS SOCIETY

There are two things that one does not talk about in England, if one is anyone at all; and these two things are sex and class. They exist, most people agree, and people have them; and that's all there is to it. There is certainly no point in making a fuss about either. The less said, the better.

Of the two, it is probably rather worse to talk about class; girls have been known to give little high-pitched screams when it is mentioned – and while a discussion about How to Have Sex in a Sexless Society might lose us a strait-laced friend or two, one on How to Have Class in a Classless Society can keep one permanently in social obloquy. When Mr Christopher Mayhew discussed the subject on television, friends looked at him narrowly and people cut him in the street; when a distinguished English sociologist was invited to lecture on the subject in America, he began his speech with 'This is a distasteful subject, and I wish I didn't have to talk about it'.

But, although it is not a subject for conversation ('It's all in your *mind*,' said one nice little girl when I attempted to explain to her that there was a class-system in England, and she rode off down the road on her pony, while I waited for the bus) and although the whole U and non-U business was completely non-U and in rather doubtful taste, every real Englishman knows deep down that class is much more important than sex. All that needs to be said about sex is this: that if Freud had not mentioned it, nobody would have found it the slightest bit interesting, and as for Freud's view that the sexual is the fundamental human drive, well, this may be true of some races one can think of but it is certainly not true of the English. Every Englishman knows that the

fundamental human drive is keeping yourself to yourself –
which is quite the opposite.

Sex is something that anyone can have, anywhere in the
world, but class, real class, you can get only in England.
Moreover, sex is strictly a night-time activity, while class
goes on all the time. Above all, you can, as our novelists
have discovered, bring class into sex – but it is impossible to
reverse the process. Thus, quite typically, we observe the
Englishman substituting an artificial for a real distinction.
Having class is, of course, the art of believing in the artificial
as something real and fundamental, and since artificial
distinctions are so much harder to maintain than real ones,
this constitutes a real challenge to the national mind. It is the
capacity to face challenges of this order that has made the
English what they are today.

If people nowadays are starting to talk about class rather
more than they used to, this is for the very obvious reason
that, as a thing diminishes, discussion of it increases. The
Education Act of 1944 has put us all on our toes about class.
There was a time, a none-too-distant time at that, when
every Englishman had a kind of personal radar which
enabled him to perceive to what class he and his interlocu-
tors belonged. It had to do with one's accent, one's clothes,
the people one knew, the place where one lived. One knew,
then, whether to defer, or be superior. Snobbery was the
thing which kept the wheels oiled. Snobbery presupposed a
clear-cut order; the snob flattered the system by imitating
the manners of those immediately above him in the scale. It
was a disease of the insecure, of those whose pretensions
exceeded their rank; and it meant that they sought to pass
above it. Snobs were never people who acted toward one in
a superior fashion and *were* superior; they were those who
did this and were not.

Thus snobbery was a largely middle-class affair; the
middle class were the people who sought to extend their
rank as their income extended itself. If you were at the
bottom you were apt to stay there; and if you were at the

top, you *were* the Joneses, and had no one to keep up with. In those days, class went, roughly speaking, with wealth and power; and one pursued all three together. But in the middle stages one found that as soon as one caught up with one lot of Joneses there were another lot just around the corner. You just had to keep on, remembering that the difference between a peerage and the bankruptcy court was a hair's breadth. The middle classes read books of etiquette to see how decent people behaved; the middle classes were genteel because they were afraid; the middle class spoke of Having Manners; the middle class were careful of their grammar (bad grammar is proper for the lower class, because they know no better, and the upper class, because they do and everyone knows that they do, even if they don't). Meanwhile, the upper classes, rightly perceiving that something is exclusive only as long as other people want to get in, and think perhaps they can, maintained their exclusiveness by assimilating a few upward strivers from time to time. But these were the good old days; nowadays there is room at the top simply because so few people want to be there.

After all, remember, a social climber is a person whose climbing is visible; and today one can't see them any more. Things have changed; England is in flux; no one behaves the way one expects them to any more. One has only to glance at the magazines formerly directed to persons of rank. Only the other day I observed in one of those glossy magazines, where everyone is photographed on horseback, that in a series describing the houses of the best people, with photographs of the hole where the Victorian wing was before it was torn down, there was an account of a visit to the home of Bessie Braddock – with photographs, as glossy as ever, of her darning her husband's underpants and so on. One thought of all those nice people reading it, and how they must have felt.

The fact is, of course, that you can't docket people any more. Fools blame the Labour Party, but of course the Labour Party is just as fond of class as everyone else. They are just as keen to preserve the old working class, with its fine old cultural heritage of making rhubarb wine and fetching its gin from the jug and bottle, and all those other splendid Richard Hoggarty things it always did before television, as the other party is to make it as sunny as it was before 1914, when the people in the first-class carriages really were first class.* The Conservative Party may have its Edwardian wilderness; the Labour Party has its William Morris wilderness.

No, the classless society is sneaking up on us unawares, and coming from a very different source, which is called mass-culture. There was a time when there was one kind of marmalade for the upper class, and one for the middle and one for the lower class. But the old-fashioned high-class goods – marmalades that cost a shilling more because all the oranges came from the north side of the hill – for the carriage trade are disappearing, and the magazines and newspapers that were divided by class boundaries are simply not any more – there are people who read *The Lady*, and are not (and what is worse, don't even want to be); while ladies often read *Woman*. Vogue is not what *Vogue* is in. Indeed, as the advertisements for *The Times* admit, anyone can be a top person now, simply by subscribing to that paper; one doesn't even have to read it – only carry it. I can remember the days when shops were run by people who knew at once how much deference to give; now you can go into shops where the only people there are store detectives in disguise.

In short, the simple means one once had of telling – or displaying – class are fading, and one even comes across people who stare at you blankly and simply *don't know*. The young are the ones who carry the burden, of course; the

---

* Nowadays, of course, the social function of the first-class carriage has quite gone; once all the people one detested were separated from one – they were, according to one's point of view, all in the third-, or in the first-class carriages.

country is swarming with the socially mobile young, who don't know what class they belong to, and hardly know which sex. We can all of us remember how easy it all was in the *old* days. In the face of this situation, where everyone is mobile and there *is* room at the top, provided you can find where the top is, even the old-fashioned standby of accent ceases to be the key. We have reached the stage of cultural hodge-podge where all accents, and all classes, seem accessible. In such a situation, guidance is needed. A new organization (Room-at-the-Top, Limited) is being formed, designed to help persons uncertain of their place in the world to conform to the values of the environment in which they choose to live (problems like when to wear check shirts, desert boots, etc., are being studied and the results tabulated). In the meantime, some interim advice on How to Have Class in a Classless Society, and which class to have, is sure to be helpful. Remember, class can be *fun* – or hell.

*

Although America is known, quite properly, as a democratic country, one cannot help noticing among Americans a somewhat undemocratic fascination with the English upper classes. Ever since the days, towards the end of the last century, when the American demi-monde was deluged with persons from England who claimed to be of blue blood, seeking to marry American girls who claimed to be heiresses, Americans have been disposed to show a special fondness for the British aristocrat; a glance at the advertisement columns of the *New Yorker* will make the point quite clear. In those halcyon days, the American press even went so far as to publish lists of eligible heiresses, with the amount of their fortunes, for the aid of these visitors; and trading a dowry for a title became one of the staples of Anglo-American commercial activity. Frequently the parties had neither and the result was, more or less, a draw.

Indeed, one rather suspects that Americans think more of

the English aristocracy than the English do themselves. This is understandable. People feel about class systems the way they do about marriage; those who are out want to get in, and those who are in want to get out. The English are on the inside of the class system and the Americans are not; they have the advantage of feeling that they are all natural aristocrats, who, if they wished, would enter in at the top rung of any European class structure. The difference actually is that the English have a class system and everybody knows about it; whereas the Americans have a class system but nobody knows about it. Every Englishman has class, because you have to live somewhere, talk some way, wear something and marry someone. People know at once. This takes the work out of class.

Americans have class but they have it in secret. This is what Mr Vance Packard overlooks when he tells us that American society is class-ridden. The American class system is called Fraternities, the Country Club, the Episcopalian church, or whatever; and instead of being administered by the Queen it is administered by sociologists. To change your class in America all you need in most cases is more IN-FORMATION. More money as well, at times; but especially more information. In America there is confusion; there are classes and you can choose. This means that class is very hard work.

Let me put the difference in this way. In England there developed a parlour game called U and non-U (U standing for upper class), to be played by non-U people. Certain manners and life-styles were defined as U, and non-U people, with all of that worthy snobbery on which any successful class system is based, had to imitate the U manners, the winners (usually Trades Union leaders) being awarded life-peerages, which are of little use to anyone. It didn't make them U, of course, because the U people know one another intimately and watch who is born very carefully indeed; but it did help to stimulate that striving for the top on which esteem for the aristocracy depends, a striving which has been waning sadly in recent years. The equivalent American game is In and Out, and the thing is local; the big wheels of Harvard are the squares of Venice, California, and in some quarters it is In to be Out and Out to be In. If you don't like the class system in America, or in your set, you can start one of your own. The latest class system is called the Beat Generation, and the rules for entry are very, very strict indeed. The only necessity is that some people should be included and others left out; and as soon as those who are out want to get in, a class system forms. In some American sets it is in to be a WASP (which means, of course, White Anglo-Saxon Protestant) and in others you have to be a white negro in order to gain entry.

Americans obtain class by information. The English find it difficult to change class because they don't know what the manners of the other classes are. Americans, on the other hand, can be anything they wish; all cultures and manners are at their disposal, and they can pick one. What they do, usually, is to hide at the centre of normalcy – at the centre of statistics, sociological curves, Kinsey reports. This is why, in America, the communications industry, and sociology, are so important. Take for example the matter of face cloths, which are always provided, at all class levels, for guests – because the magazines say you should . . . say that it is normal. In a recent issue of an American magazine named *McCall's*, famed for its gospel of togetherness ('The family that prays together stays together'), an article called 'Are Your Habits Normal?' explained to American conformists to what they had to conform. Anyone who has read modern American novels will be under the impression that Americans spend much of their time enjoying nude bathing parties (while Erskine Caldwell hides in the bushes with a tape recorder) but we now learn that out of 100 million American adults only 32 million men and 10 million women have gone swimming in the nude. Thus nude bathing is not normal, a whole 8 million away from being normal. It is also abnormal to strike one's husband under provocation (only one woman in five has ever done it); moreover, to be normal, you have to eat three-quarters of a ton of food annually, have foot trouble, swallow about once a minute, sigh every three of four minutes, and spend eleven to fourteen per cent of your waking hours in darkness, because you're blinking. The point of such surveys is that those who don't already, will.

The people who administer the Pursuit of Normalcy are the sociologists. Sociologists are, of course, people who use the same material as novelists, but *do a random sample first*. There are times when, looking first at little children and then at sociologists, one feels that sociology is the only true innocence; then, looking first at the world and then at sociology, one feels that it is the only true depravity. There was a time before sociology, when society used to be itself, and *not know about it*. The numbers of men in upper income groups marrying women in upper income groups had more than random significance, but few realized it; that was life. There was a time when there was class and nobody knew that class was what it was, or that things could be otherwise, or that you could talk about it. Even in these days it still seems hard for sociologists to admit that there was once a whole world with no sociologists in it, yet full of sociological things, elaborately patterned societies that must have organized themselves. In England we have never taken sociology too seriously, presumably on the grounds that one does not start taking the 'plane to pieces before it leaves the ground; but things may well be changing.

The other curious thing about sociology is that, unlike all other academic disciplines, it is always right. Sociologists can never hurt themselves. This is called Being the Joneses; they are the ones with whom everyone else keeps up. They are, to themselves, an aristocracy; whatever they do is always U because they can always explain it. However they furnish their houses, it is a symbol of something.

The best illustration I can think of is folk music. It is all right to love folk music if you are not folk, stuck with it as your culture; by coming around full circle, by going away from your roots and then looking back on them at a distance with a *sociological* interest, you can like it again. The same is true of hand-woven tweeds, old cars, Victorian bric-à-brac. Given sufficient distance from their original use, these things become cultural objects to be used again. This view of them is sociological (it is the view often held in the Labour Party about working-class culture). When we are all sufficiently *déclassé* and far enough from our roots to be objective about things, we will all become sociologists. The consequence of being de-culturalized is to be able to have all cultures, without being completely involved in any one. This is the ultimate sociological view. This is how to have class in a classless society. Thus it is fine to possess horse brasses so long as no one thinks that you're a carter. It is splendid to have a working-class accent if you work in a university, and it is grand to wear tattered clothes if you are a lord.

This is the simple answer to the quandary of declining class in England. You can have the manners of any group so long as you do it sociologically. Let us look at an example. A follower came to Room-at-the-Top Limited with a quandary; he had acquaintance of all class levels and was not, in fact, sure what class he himself belonged to. He was about to marry, buy a house and a car; but he did not want to be committed to a particular class level. We advised him as follows: marry a foreigner (an American was our suggestion), buy one of those German cars with the engine at the back, which (because of import duty) cost more than they should; and live in a cottage furnished with Victoriana. All of these suggestions were *hostile*. That is to say, none of the goods could be priced, and none had any specific class associations. Moreover, since he spent more on the car than he could afford, and less on his furniture, people were hard put to classify him. He prospered financially, retains the same car, house and wife, and spends entirely on non-essentials – unnecessary visits to America (which can be explained, to those of his friends who would dislike him if they felt he were rich, as 'business'), expensive wines (which can be described as 'cheap' to those who don't know) and so on. He has desocialized himself completely, the ultimate sociological aim. Nobody knows who he is and that, in England, is quite something.

*

The important thing to remember about English life is that all situations are (at least potentially) class situations. Everyone has his place, and can be put in it. The English do not have friends, but superiors, inferiors, and equals. Without this orientation, one is either naïve, or an American. Americans are endlessly amused by the fact that English people talk to one another about the weather, when they talk at all; in fact, there is a sound reason for this (beside custom, which is a sound enough reason for anyone), and that is that weather is one of the few (discussable) experiences common to all classes. In addition, by talking about the weather, one can learn quickly the accent of the other person and decide whether one wants to have a conversation at all. And while most American novels are about the American experience, and what it's like not to know who you are, and how it feels to have sex (or hit somebody – which is, for Americans, much the same thing), most English novels are about the experience of a particular social stratum, and what it's like to know too well who you are, and how it feels to have class. If Americans are constantly seeking to find identity, the English are only too keen to lose it. One of the discoveries of the modern novel has been that there are, in England, people who change their shirts every day – that's what all the new novels seem to be about. It is, of course, a class discovery, and from it you may learn that authors, as a group, are changing; at one time authors were upper middle class, and dedicated their books to so-and-so, in whose garden this book was written, and they would never have dreamed of writing of people who changed their shirts every day, because they assumed, naturally, that everybody did.

Whenever two Englishmen meet, on a desert island or in the heart of America, they set up a pecking order to see who defers to whom. Notice the word 'Whoops!' It is a significant cry. All over the world, in hotel lounges and in the dining-rooms of ocean liners, you will meet dear old English ladies, laden with knitting, and you will come through a door one way as she is coming through it the other; and she will cry, not 'Sorry!', but 'Whoops!' This has the function of delaying apologies until the class orientations of the situation are apparent, when the inferior person, whether responsible for the situation or not, will then say 'Sorry!' There are old ladies from Dower Houses who can go through life without ever having to feel guilty about having done anything. These are persons of quality, and the thing about quality is that if you have it, all mistakes are other people's. Even when finances are low, respect remains; there are always the respectful middle-class nurse-type women who know gentlefolk when they see them (the sort who say: 'I nursed Lady X to the finish; she had a beautiful end'; and 'Were you at Oxford? My favourite university!'). Persons who think that monarchy is without influence should be aware of the effect that it has on such persons, the salt of the earth, who know the family trees of all the nobility and spend much of their time commenting on how like her grandfather the young duchess of this or that is. Remember Jane Austen's condemnation of her character, Frank Churchill: 'His indifference to a confusion of rank bordered too much on inelegance of mind.'

The fact remains that quality is not to be had by all of us. It is not even proper, always, to aim for it. There are few classes nowadays that you cannot get into by your own efforts, but the quality is one of them (the working class, likewise a cabal, is the other). You may be knighted, but it is your grandson who will be quality; one generation cannot accomplish the task, and for this reason we are inclined to recommend to most people that they set their sights lower.

Our advice to persons intent on choosing a class is: decide what class to be, and stick to it. Do not aim too high too soon. Nowadays, more than ever, you can choose; but choose carefully. It is so easy to get out of your depth in these things. Never drop names or hold values that you cannot substantiate. This looks like snobbery, and while snobbery is flattering for others it is demeaning to you. After all, every class is, in its different way, rewarding. There are certain environments in which there is real *cachet* in being working class and sticking to it. Some of these can be briefly listed:

> Universities, pigeon-fancying, libraries, horse-racing, B.B.C. Light Programme, novel-writing, railway station announcing, *The Times*, the Conservative Party.

In the following environments, on the other hand, it is better to be upper class:

> Universities, pigeon-fancying, libraries, horse-riding, B.B.C. Light Programme, novel-writing, railway station announcing, the *Daily Mirror*, the Labour Party.

There is, it has to be admitted, little kudos in claiming that one is middle class nowadays, especially if one actually belongs to it, which, of course, most of us do. If one cannot actually claim powerful aristocratic connections, we recommend the traditional custom of devaluing one's parents, and making them appear to be of working-class background; there is plenty of contemporary reading matter available to assist you in this perfectly harmless pretence. It has the advantage of making it clear how hard you have worked to get where you are, while at the same time giving evidence of the fact that you do not really belong there. The important thing to remember is that, while the British have always admired both the honest working man and the eccentric Milord, they have never admired what lies in between. The word 'bourgeois' is one of the most unpleasant of insults, regularly applied by writers, artists and politicians from middle-class backgrounds (like, for example, that exemplary bourgeois Karl Marx) to other people from middle-class backgrounds. Much of English literature is based on the assumption that the middle classes like to read books accusing them of being stuffy, money-making, self-engrossed and poor in spirit; and this has always proved to be true. There is just a *very* slight possibility that the middle classes may be coming back, now that the sociologists are showing signs of turning their attention in this direction. Thus, fresh from their study of real, honest back-to-back Bethnal Green, Peter Wilmott and Michael Young have lately been wandering the well-knapped lawns of Woodford. Naturally there was the first aversion to overcome ('East End children do not trot their ponies along forest paths wearing hunting caps, East End houses do not have stone gnomes in their back-yards'), but there comes a moment when Wilmott seems to soften a little, Young to grow somewhat more gentle. Perhaps it was the absence of violence, the presence of neatness and cleanliness; perhaps it was that the British still respect the underdog when they see him; but there is more than a hint or two in their book that, amid the horrors, a gleam or two of decency shines.

Still, a note of suspicion remains in order. When we think of the middle classes today, we are no longer thinking of, for example, those middle-aged ladies who toured the nineteenth-century world collecting flowers and plants to bring home to their English gardens, and who appeared round every pyramid and temple from Egypt to the Far East, speaking English very loudly so that the foreigners could understand it. Now the middle classes are the universal Joneses, endlessly keeping up with themselves. You can see them on their patios in their sun-loungers drinking drinks with ice in, or sitting in red sports cars with foulard scarves tucked in the necks of their open shirts, before returning to their modernized cottage in the Kentish village where the thatched shop specializes in antiques. In their living room, the Danish furniture gleams as he works the Sodastream while she prepares the lasagne and courgettes. The new middle class is the slightly-better-than-average viewer, the just-above-typical housewife, the up-market consumer; all you need is a red setter and a Volvo, and you are as good as there.

There is one further group membership of which is well worth considering; we will in fact be returning to them later. These are the outsiders – those persons who see themselves as being quite outside the entire British class structure, living in radical rebellion and alienation. It is often very hard to distinguish them from the groups mentioned last, as they usually eat their lasagne and courgettes and strip their pine furniture in very much the same sort of way. In fact what distinguishes them is that, when you talk to them, you will discover that they describe themselves as writers, or painters or artists; this does not mean that they, write, paint, or art, but that they like that sort of life, with its bohemian associations, its aura of virtuous poverty and vague sexual impropriety. Frequently assisted by private incomes, gov-ernmental largesse or a working spouse, they profess an air of social suffering while actually being able to afford not to work, as most of us cannot. Naturally they are not particu-larly admired by those who do possess one sort of niche or another in the social mechanism, and this may put you off the life. However, there is quite a lot to be said for being socially mobile in this way *for a while*, because a period like this – a couple of years weaving rugs, for example – is an ideal way of obscuring one's actual class origins, and finally one can fit into life wherever one pleases – when, that is, one comes to one's senses at last. It is not at all a bad way of doing things, because the outsider is always a useful source of disquiet, and in any case it is a classic way of the world

98

that the sceptic and the critic is always finally given a seat on the committee, if only to shut him up.

The real, professional subterranean has begun his trade early in life; if he has had a proper start his name and existence will not have been registered at birth and the army and the government will have no papers to prove that he exists, however much they may suspect it. This demands a quality of foresight among parents unfortunately wanting in our day and age. If one has friends or parents, one is damned from the start; one has at least to run away to another town and begin under a new name – a procedure fraught with difficulties in these days when one has national health cards, and income tax histories. Wives can be rebelled against, as Mr Osborne has shown us, particularly if they are inoffensive and dulled middle-class women. But this demands an initial alienation which is, alas, not too easily come by nowadays.

Don't feel, however, that we are putting difficulties in your way. By spending the night out on Hampstead Heath, a couple of sleeping bags down from Colin Wilson, by stealing other people's cigarettes, kicking over their dustbins and burning their bedsheets, one can do something, however little, to protest against the growing conformity of modern life. The only problem is anti-conformity conformity; bohemianism is now as fashionable a way of life as any other. Room-at-the-Top Limited has a theory going called the conformity of nonconformity, which alleges that one has only to chart out a *weltanschauung* of protest for the larger part of society to take it up. Outsiders are inside before they know what's happening to them; protest is so fashionable that everyone is doing it. The only real way to protest is to buy a thornproof suit and hide among the middle classes. You have only to go into any London espresso bar to discover that it is full of bank clerks from the suburbs, protesting for the evening by drinking real coffee and mentioning the word Nietzsche. Apparently, from their dress and manner, in dedicated conversations about stealing marbles to roll under the feet of policemen's horses, they are, in fact, worrying about how to meet the payments on their vacuum cleaners.

Moreover, outsiders overlook one thing. If one has no class one is condemned by the company that one keeps; one is condemned by default. Persons going up to Oxbridge are advised always to make no friends for the first term, in case they get mixed up with the wrong people. Once you acquire friends, or a wife, you are done for. Friend Orsler encountered an interesting example of this the other day. "I've heard so much about you," cried a woman, brightly, claiming acquaintance at a party. "Oh!" asked Orsler. "Who from?" "From Mrs Higgins," said the woman. "Oh, yes," said Orsler, inadvisedly, forgetting to be wary, as one always must be, "she's a great friend of ours." "I see," said the woman, in cooler tones. "She comes in and does for us twice a week." This is the pecking order; this is *how class works*. If you must have acquaintances, never speak of them in other company unless speaking of them confers merit – merit without ostentation.

*

It is often assumed by the liberal-minded that as wealth declines the English class structure will fade away and the man of quality will disappear for good. But persons of quality are already facing up to the basic question – how does one maintain one's class in a classless society? Since in a classless society money and class do not necessarily coincide (indeed, it is a long time since they did, so that as wealth increased, class, to save its face, became something that you could not buy but had to mature over generations; and you cannot purchase time) the need is for new markers that are not associated with wealth – for, indeed, such things as the new *post-Veblenism*.

Maintaining one's class in a classless society, if one already has it, is by no means as hardy a proposition as it might appear. Things were worse in the old days when, because there were so many classes about, one might always, in an inadvertent moment, falter in one's presentation of oneself, and so slip down the imperceptible but shiny slope into a lower class position. Nowadays one is so much better off, since the government have provided, so to speak, a minimum class level below which none shall be allowed to fall, and this minimum is a sort of rebounding board for all who are aware of the prerequisites and requirements of class. Thus, if they slip, they can, in our anonymous and mobile society, spring back again – chastened by the experience and strengthened in their resolve to put up a better show next time.

After the American social commentator Mr Thorstein Veblen noted that the leisured classes tended to display what he called their 'pecuniary eminence' by what he also called 'conspicuous consumption' (that is by overt and unnecessary display, such as white shirts and liveries for footmen), English gentlemen looked on the spectacle with disgust. They wondered how persons could be so vulgar. Americans, only, could confuse money with class, to begin with. And one does not (they felt) need to show that one is a gentleman by overt display; it shows itself, surely. A gentleman either is, or is not. And one does not show it by display but by lack of it. It is only the socially uneasy – the *nouveau riche*, and Americans – who need such trumpery, for a gentleman may live in a hovel but everyone knows from his cultivation (centuries of training) and his manners (centuries of personal relationships, an important point because, up to the nineteenth century, only the upper classes had personal relationships) and his accent (centuries of pronouncing things) that he was a gentleman. In any case, a gentleman does not boast; if there is anything to be boasted about someone else will always do it for one. Actually Veblen had noted this too, observing that the leisured classes demonstrated their leisure by indulgence in useless pursuits (personal relationships, scholarship, etc.), but gentlemen didn't read that far, because, as every gentleman knows, one buys books to have them bound, not to read them.

However, there herewith developed a new ostentatious modesty or *conspicuous inconsumption*. Everyone has heard of *in*conspicuous consumption, where your clothes cost five times as much as everyone else's but looked the same, so that only the *cognoscenti* knew – but this was conspicuous *in*consumption, and it came at a very fortunate time, a time when the upper classes were faced with the old middle-class problem of making ends meet. It was partly in answer to the problem where the gentleman needs to be distinguished from those who can afford to be gentlemen but are not, while gentlemen cannot afford to be gentlemen but are, that the new conspicuous inconsumption came into being. The subtlety involved here is that people should be able, by various means, to ascertain that a gentleman could afford to do these other things should he so wish, but that he is too distinguished to want to. If you, or I, were to expose ourselves in public (without having first established status in some way) wearing an old Harris tweed suit with loose threads and smelling of dog and sweat, and with holes in our socks and with flies undone, we would be poorly received; but any old peer may do this providing that he establish that he is a real gentleman by a fish-fly in the hat and a scattering of lead shot in the interstices of the fabric.

As this is an age of participation, and possessions are common to all classes, goods of any sort now serve little conspicuous consumption purpose. All over the American south there are dirty, untoiled shanty towns where the hovels are built of tar paper and are lived in by negroes. Outside stands a Cadillac, and the Cadillac is losing its high class association because it is a *negro's car*. The like process has taken place here. 'Ping,' goes the doorbell in high-class shops (Est. 1738, Pedigree Stock) as the gentleman goes in to order a dozen pairs of socks, and complain about people who wear belts instead of braces. But class goods are going out, except among the *nouveau riche*, and this type of shop is being pushed out by the chain store. Modom shops are still preferable, of course, but you pay 75 per cent more for the modom – and since it's not people of class who have money, off to C. and A. Modes or M. and S. (only the middle class mean Marshall and Snelgrove when they say M. and S.; the upper crust mean, of course, Marks and Spencer). The upper stratum has simply stopped setting the fashion; taste is now made by specialists. It is an industry. The newest fashion is to be unfashionable. The simple art is to buy things that are either fantastically expensive or fantastically cheap. It is the middle range one has to steer clear of. Fashion setting and novelties mark a fellow down; if you want to set fashions, simply be yourself. Someone will follow.

The new inconspicuous consumption is a fashion designed to give the impression that one is simply not bothering. The idea that is conveyed is that one is spending all one's money on significant things – on intangibles. One lives in the kind of house in which (at first sight) no one can live. 'Where's the furniture?' people are tempted to ask as they enter. Sitting on the floor can be fun, after all. Bare woodwork, with a termite or two, and open brickwork, are in vogue. This is called *au naturel*; a better name would be outdoor living, indoors. Remember, the more you possess, the more quickly your room dates. And it is fashionable to appear underprivileged. Have, therefore, bookcases made from planks and bricks. Table lamps made from beer bottles. A hi-fi *with all the wires showing*, and trailing all over the house, so that people trip as they enter the door. Pictures are dating, and fads change so quickly; better to have wall posters, begged from Cooks, with messages like SEE FRANCE BY GERMAN RAILWAYS. If a car, an old crock that looks as though it was built to be pulled by a horse. Above all, *cacti* (remember, succulents are a form of puritanism, and suggest spiritual austerity, the mood you are trying to convey). The impression given by all this is that you have contracted out of the business of being fashionable and are leaving it to the *canaille*; and no one will blame you if you live elsewhere and use this establishment simply in order to entertain guests.

It is to be observed that gentlefolk to the Manor born have their own way of life now. Thus the author was on board a vessel, in the tourist class, with a dowager lady of quality, Lady X. A remarkable eccentric, who spent the voyage doing the stations of the cross in the bows and stern of the vessel in high gales, she still maintained status without income. When she was not bombarding her landlord with letters begging him to allow her to live rent-free in her dwelling, she spent her time being incompetent and needing help. Everyone had tasks which she designated to them – woolwinding, cleaning her shoes, fetching her broth. Parts of the ship unavailable to others were open to her. When forms were to be filled in she had no knowledge of how to fill them; there were, she was aware, people who did know, and they did them. It was her custom to remark, as she sat in the lounge painting water colours of flower gardens in Dorset, her face blue with the paint she had transferred to it, 'We're all charladies now. I spend all my time in my apron.' No doubt she did, but there is equally no doubt that she was so incompetent that someone else did the actual charring, as a favour. I was thinking of her when I remarked at a lecture in America that the upper classes have no money but live as if they had. Afterwards a member of the audience told me the story of meeting, on a ship, an upper-class lady who had to travel tourist, and whom she and other Americans regularly smuggled up into the first-class for dinner. She then asked me how such people lived. They lived, I explained, by being permanently smuggled up into the first-class for dinner.

There was a time, after all, when there were only two real classes – Really Top Drawer, and A Bit Frayed at the Heels. Now that the two are one, the gentleman is really put on his mettle. Suffice it to say that he is responding with true *noblesse*.

PART FOUR

HAVING QUALITY

Every person of quality knows, more or less instinctively, that there are certain senses in which the whole idea of class is a pure invention, something that has been brought about by morbid and continued introspection on the subject by so-called 'specialists'. These persons are themselves a symptom of the neurosis of our time. There was a time, not so long ago, when these things did not matter in the same way as they are now supposed to matter, and then people were not concerned about what class they were, and what they ought to feel about it. They simply 'carried on' in the best British tradition. Even people of no quality at all were much happier, being content to be at the other end of *noblesse oblige*. And so they might – collecting their maundy money and their Queen's shilling with a merry air.

It is certainly true that class consciousness today is a totally proletarian phenomenon. People of quality are not conscious of class – they may know the crowd they run with, but they do not think in terms of class. No one is so preoccupied with class as those who have not got it. They seem most concerned with something which is called 'social mobility'. This is nothing new; it is just 'getting on', and the most important aspect of it, according to the texts, is acquiring a better job than one's father, and marrying a richer woman than one's mother. These principles have been known to the aristocracy for centuries, but they have recently been discovered by sociologists who have now sought to make the public aware of them; indeed, they are the principal selling line of these merchants. Of course, the crude emphasis on getting a better job than one's father is just a modern technologized version of Oedipus, a way of doing him down. The marriage side of it is more complicated. There was a time when beauty was a principal criterion in picking a mate, but today ugly women have disappeared so alarmingly that there is really scarcely any criterion in choosing a wife except her fortune.

Since social mobility has become so popular, it is necessary for people of good stock to know a little more about their own position in this regard. For the general public it is clear that there was ever only one direction for them in which to be mobile (the process is often painfully slow, despite the vivid terminology) and clearly for the aristocracy too there is only one way to go, and this is downwards. It becomes self-evidently clear then that people who really matter are either not mobile at all, or are discreetly and gently mobile in a downwards direction.

Indelicate as the subject is, the question of 'making ends meet in a classless society' is one which many gentlefolk in reduced circumstances must face. Income tax with Pitt, death duties at the end of the nineteenth century, 'progressive taxation' – all these form the background of the present difficulties of people of quality. None of these measures was understood in in its full import at the time of introduction, and proceeded on the theoretically and apparently unobjectionable assumption that small, organized re-distributions would greatly assist the condition of the less fortunate classes. Clearly the process has got out of hand, and the subsidizing of the masses by the classes has become the rule in the modern state, reducing the classes to a parlous condition, in which their culture and way of life stands likelihood of being totally eroded.

There are, however, still means to enable those with culture and breeding to continue in the style of life to which they – or their forebears – have been accustomed. Large houses which cannot be maintained can be given over to voluntary bodies, for which ex-owners can be Wardens, Organizing Secretaries or Honorary Presidents. Since priwatte domestic service has disappeared, domestics must be recruited through the bureaucracy. The State is the only establishment wealthy enough to maintain domestic service, and although the quality has deteriorated and the personal allegiance is lost, it is still as a vestige something like the style of things in time past. In an age of extravagance a gentleman must be a man who, without any penny-pinching or purse-carrying, such as was in the last century the hallmark of the Primitive Methodist, is nonetheless a man of careful economy. Waste is not gentlemanly, and such is the condition of our lingering Debretted classes that they cannot afford it anyway. But even in the heyday of people of quality, vulgar extravagance was to be eschewed; it was typical of the newly risen financiers, diamond millionaires, scrap merchants, market manipulators, lathe-turners, colliery workers, film stars and guitar-strummers.

In any case, if there is one thing above another which marks a fellow down in this world, it is striving for things new. Novelty is never acceptable to a person of class . . . . even new clothes are the mark of the parvenu. Everything – but everything – about a person of quality should have the stamp of being familiar. He should be used to his obviously good-quality clothes, used to his once quality car, used to his riding breeches and boots (and they, of course, should be used to him). One cannot set up as a person of quality overnight – one must *use* oneself into the role. Consequently new things and novelties strike a false note. Much better to have that old, slightly faded, dog-eared look, and carry it off with courtly *aplomb*. Remember of clothes that texture is always more important than colour, and of cars that comfort is always more important than speed. The reference to clothes and cars is a concession to the world. There was a day when a gentleman was known by his clothes, and he still may be, in terms of their age and their well-cared-for look, but no longer, alas, by the simple device of expensive cut and styling. These things belong now to a totally different class in society; fortunately, *they* are interested only in new things, and although they have taken the outward and visible manifestations of wealth and prestige, they lack, as they always must, the inward and invisible grace which, to the discerning eye, is the mark of the true gentleman, 'to the Manor born'.

Likewise in the question of furnishing your house; it is just as well to maintain a slightly shabby look. Shabbiness, you must remember, is never really out of fashion, and it is so easy to maintain. Shiny things are taboo, as being the mark of the vulgar, hygienic bourgeoisie. Oddments of old furniture are to be specially prized: contrived splendour is no longer possible to those who really matter. Even in personal appearance the shades of cosmetics which give that slightly faded look all serve to enhance the association with past glories. There is nothing so fashionable as the old-fashioned. Within moderation, of course.

Increasingly there is a risk that these days people will stop you in the street and want to know highly personal matters about you and your family. People of quality, providing they have the time, will not mind this sort of innocent incursion into their affairs by an increasingly inquisitive public. After all, it is part of one's lot, and this is the modern way in which the general public acknowledge their social betters, now that balcony appearances and the pleasant pomp of earlier ages has disappeared. There is, of course, no obligation to take these things too seriously. One may tell them what one thinks they want to hear, which is very courteous: or one may tell them what one thinks the truth ought to be, which is also a way of acting on principle. Dignity, of course, is essential, and nothing should induce one to reveal closer matters. As a rule of thumb it is as well to be open and frivolous about sex, correct and punctilious, but not enthusiastic, about The Church, sceptical of politics, but high-minded about The Turf. One should never reveal anything about one's income except to deny it, and never accept relationships with anyone except county families, since people in cities are not usually worth knowing.

One should add that at a time of threat to national culture, to the survival of a way of life which has developed slowly over centuries, and which has within it the very truths of destiny, it is all the more vital that the pristine qualities of the gentleman should be preserved. The mark of quality is today in need of support, and every surrender to the casual and easy virtue of indiscriminate generosity can only result in the loss of every vestige of class. No one should suppose that classlessness means anything other than the elimination of the quality of class — a levelling which previously we have, correctly, left to the efficient and timely operation of death.

*

Maintaining one's class in a classless society is by no means as difficult as it might appear. Self-possession is the cardinal virtue of a gentleman, and, naturally enough, self-possession comes from the possession of other people. The latter is now not so easy in a literal sense, but one can do it with a few simple turns of phrase. Always relate yourself to both objects and people, and always do so in the position of superiority, by possessing them. You will say, for instance, "My postman tells me . . . ." This simply oozes confidence, and expresses the reality of your own position in the world. "Oh, I shall take my usual train to town tomorrow . . ." conveys a strong sense of one's importance, even though one knows that literally the train will take you, that it is not really yours, and that it will go to town whether you do or not — nonetheless in the inner recesses of your mind and in that of your hearer your superiority, your ability to command and to decide has been firmly established. This is terribly good for you as a man of quality, and who can doubt that it is also fearfully good for others, who know quite assuredly now whom they should look up to as a superior. In personal relations, this general ability to possess can be re-emphasized by occasionally addressing people as "My dear fellow" (for friends), "My good chap" (for acquaintances), and 'My good man' (for tradespeople and civil servants).

There are, in fact, certain speech patterns which are the mark of the real gentleman. 'Look here,' you will find yourself saying, with all the descending (and condescending) cadences, and perfunctory pronunciation of consonants, which characterize a person thoroughly used to being looked at, and *to*. The imperative is the mood in which one should live most of the time. It saves time, it sets the tone for the way things are to be done, and it saves a lot of wishy-washy discussion which leads nowhere. With care the imperative can be introduced into almost every statement. '*Do* come here,' you will say, '*Do* let me say this . . .' or 'Let me repeat again . . .' All this adds weight, dignity, aplomb to the things you have to say. It always helps if you do really have something to say as well, but this is by no means essential. Many gentlemen have managed quite well without ever having anything to say at all; the secret is that, although they have had nothing to say, they have said it emphatically and well.

Contrary to the naïve assumptions of social climbers, every person of quality knows, by instinct, by learning, even by hard experience, that his position ultimately rests on good relations with the lower orders. It is not the absence of association with people of lower classes which has established the real man of class, but rather the type and character of his association with them. Particularly in a classless society, it is more than ever necessary for those with class to cultivate those with less. This is not a courtesy, but a necessity: good-quality associates one can always find, but a char, a gardener, a butler – these are the salt of the earth. There is no greater mistake than to treat these people on equal terms. Patronage is absolutely necessary if one is to succeed, and this should consist of the calculated and occasional extension of particular privileges. One must treasure the intimacy that one can establish with such people, and it is very necessary to talk of it to everyday contacts. Nothing establishes one's own superiority better than the pride one obviously takes in the privileged intimacy one has with the lower orders, and even with the less desirable elements of society. After all, only those with enormous security of status can really afford to reveal their contact with people much lower down the scale. The class-less society even helps one here, and for those who really know how to use the opportunities of a welfare state, there was never a time when one could so easily establish one's pre-eminence, by condescending to associate with the generality from time to time.

A man of class has the enormous advantage in contemporary life of never really needing to know anything very well. The cultivation of an amiable vagueness, and a willingness to listen to, and hence to patronize, those with specialist knowledge, are all that are necessary. One of the modern tokens of rank is to regard everything that is currently happening as temporary, or as a momentary aberration. Vagueness is a great defence, but also the best guarantee to outsiders that one does no particular thing to justify one's existence in the world, except be oneself. One gives the impression that one can always rely on the knowledge of others, should occasion demand; one should be an amateur, a gentleman amateur, but know specialists. 'You're a brain,' you say to them. 'You tell me . . .' Particularly for those class members interested in politics this rule is very necessary. There is nothing that has contributed to political failure more than knowing too much. Vagueness also helps in terms of one's dissociation from the everyday world. One must display a certain conspicuous ignorance, as if one were never exposed to mass media, and as if one's life were lived in a world utterly remote from the everyday affairs and concerns of lesser classes. It is particularly unwise to admit to knowledge of any popular contemporary figures in the world of entertainment, except those who confine themselves to more exclusive night clubs (if any such there now be). The shadow world of television must certainly never be given substance by conferring on it, or its doyens, any semblance of recognition. 'Huw who? . . . What does he do? . . . Local chap is he? . . . No, never heard of him.' One must always make it clear that the things which are seen by the people are not part of the lives of the classes. Failure on this issue means the loss of a valuable mystique. Popular illusions on this subject are vital both to the upper crust and the general public, who without some such notion would probably lose all faith and confidence in people of the better sort.

Although one cultivates a vagueness toward popular surgings, one must not deride the manifestations of progress. They may be given the general connotation of irrelevance to real life, but never opposed. Many noble families have sealed their own fates by open hostility to change and mass developments. It is an understandable but lamentably short-sighted policy. After all there is nothing more characteristic of the gentleman than that he does not get involved with things. Quality people do not get tense, alarmed or seriously disturbed. This is left for strivers on the one hand and intellectuals on the other. One remains above the fray, and although one is certainly not in favour of progress, one simply assumes the sanity of others' point of view – one simply does not argue about these things. Argument, as a titled lady once observed, disturbs the composure, and sometimes even makes one doubt one's own mission in life. For people of class this will never do. And just as one refuses to become anxious about the contemporary world, so one must never display concern about status. The struggle for status is beneath the man of class, who assumes himself at the top. Likewise one should always remain unaffected by passing fashion, by the know-how of the contemporary world, for one's position rests rather on insulation from these things than from association with them. Fashions, being temporary, are dangerous to people whose position must be firmly associated and identified with the durable and permanent things of life. To some extent one must 'keep up'; there is no objection to having a car for instance. Most persons of quality cannot drive, but do. This is a proper mixture.

This is not to say that class position should in any sense inhibit the individual from the cultivàtion of distinctive tastes; quite the reverse. But one's hobby should be carefully selected. It must not be commonplace, and certainly not expensive. Nor should it be scholarly. A gentleman, unlike most of the'young men of today, knows that nothing much is to be got from one's education. Knowledge never got anyone anywhere. The sort of education of real value to a gentleman is one which involves abundant leisure. Long looking at pictures, tasting of wine, eating of food (and the ability to withstand lots of it, richly cooked, without evident discomfort) are virtues to be cultivated. One need not have a catholic taste in art, and the ability to sit still and look interested is all one needs for music. In general the day when musical performances were obligatory for the gentry has gone: very few people these days seem to maintain their own string orchestras, and it is not often that this sort of entertainment will be offered. As one gentleman, who was in his day an authority on county matters, declared, 'Music is a bore . . . but it sometimes saves you from conversation which is even more of a bore.' Enthusiasm for music, or for anything very much, is difficult to combine with the true marks of class. People of class are not enthusiasts, as one must never admit to having 'hobbies'. Nothing should develop into an over-riding preoccupation, or get into the way of things, a gentleman really should want to do. Hunting prints, good portraits, landscapes – preferably English eighteenth- and nineteenth-century pictures (since the complicated people who paint nowadays seem unable to keep themselves out of their pictures and some dreadful entanglements ensue) – these are always safe. But too close a concern for these things lays a man open to suspicion of Intellectualism or, worse, of his drawing his livelihood from them. Such things are not for persons of quality.

Finally, the gentleman of today need never be financially

embarrassed, except by surfeit. Money long ago ceased to be really fashionable in a man of quality, and we can assume this fashion is here to stay. Brutal frankness about lack of money is always to be recommended, especially concerning those types of expenditure which are now thoroughly common to the masses. One simply cannot afford a television set – this one must constantly affirm. No one, of course, believes it, but they are so relieved that you are kind enough to say so, rather than to pour contempt on their uninnocent recreations. Of course, when one makes such a comment, there must not be the slightest twinge – but not the slightest – of resentment; otherwise one runs the risk that people might think what one says is true.

PART FIVE

LIVING IN THE PRESENT

Thus, to sum up so far: in the beginning, God created the Heaven and the Earth. And darkness there was on the face of the earth. Then God said, let there be light, and there was light. And then He created the beasts of the field, and the fish that swam in the seas. He then created human beings; and these He divided into two sexes, male and female, expecting that this would prove a popular arrangement, which, indeed, it did, except in some quarters. Therefore, after further thought, he created the English, and these He divided into nine classes: lower working, middle working, and upper working; lower middle, middle middle and upper middle; lower upper, middle upper, and upper upper. And this, especially with the English, proved an even more popular arrangement. For sex was a private, night-time, and intensely personal, if not unpleasant, activity, which one kept quiet about; whereas class could be done in public, at all hours of the day and night, and could be talked about, enjoyed, and exploited in every field of behaviour. For generation after generation, this entire arrangement worked very well, making the English the distinctive and remarkable race they are. Then, however, came the mid twentieth-century, not a good idea, and things began somewhat to change.

At first the English did not recognize this change, and many of them still do not. They maintained their traditional customs and values, asserted their classic values, and went on much as they always had. In America and other curious countries, strange things were occurring; accustomed to the solidity of their own characters and the sturdy familiarity of their own lives, the British merely smiled. They noted the obsession with goods, the disappearance of privacy, the obsessive need for psychology (as if there was something else inside a person besides organs and guts), the endless soul-searching, the chatter about me, the clustering of people into groups, hungering for togetherness, the ceaseless probing of society, the unremitting, boring desire to know who and what one actually was. To all these questions the British found the answers quite clear, and they had no truck with them whatsoever, going on in the old way, if not more so. But then came the 1950s, and the first uneasy signs of change. Symptoms began to show everywhere. Glass-walled office blocks started to appear in the streets, washing machines and consumer durables in the stores, Danish furniture in the homes of people one had always understood to be perfectly reliable, commercials on the television, showing silly anxious wives worrying about getting their whites white enough, a demeaningly lower-middle-class sort of preoccupation. Little pretentious moustaches started appearing on people's faces; chaps turned up for the office in clothes only fit for the golf-course. Young people weren't young people any more; sociologists started to appear, trying to explain society as if it were not self-evident; and worst of all, people started talking to other people about their problems.

Thus, when, in the late 1950s, we returned home, Orsler from the Orient, Bradbury from the United States, and looked around to inspect what had been going on in our absence, it was immediately apparent to both of us that things were in process of change. It was not hard to avoid the suspicion that, taking advantage of our departure, the British had decided to turn themselves into a nation of consumers on the world model. We had left an England that had been a bastion of phogey commonsense, a land that insisted the British would never take to such things as rock and roll, the hoola hoop, or the commercial selling of goods. Now, though, something seemed to have happened. For one thing, something seemed to have attenuated national pride.

People were apologizing for being British, in ways they never had before, and it was apparent that in no time at all they would be worrying about the perils of conformity, the problems of the shook-up generation and the waist-high culture, and all sorts of other new and fashionable socio-logical anxieties of exactly the kind I had just left behind me in the United States. Evidently they were right to do so; for you had only to go into the Old Tar's bar of the local pub (even the bars, it seemed, were being done over in the spirit of sentimental modernism) to find people filling out their hire-purchase agreements, worrying about what their next need would be, wondering what identity to have after this one, and in general manifesting all the symptoms of being modern men.

Indeed, on all sides, the crudest of modern desires, desire for membership of the present, was displaying itself. The Englishman of the old style, so carefully analysed in pre-vious chapters, was still everywhere in evidence, of course, and will doubtless remain so. But also in evidence was a strange new sort of fellow, an apparently imported brand of person to whom no one would have dreamed of allowing space in the country a few years earlier – an American sort of person, who assumed that if life went wrong, one could always start again, under one's own name or another, and that it was perfectly proper to shop around for the right sort of social system until one found one that was to one's taste, who assumed, in short, that anyone could be anything. Thus the signs were that strange Oedipal compulsions were rife, even in Britain; on right and left, there were English people who were symbolically killing their fathers, departing from their old rôles, investing in unheard-of psychic novelties. There could be little doubt about it; even in Britain, the modern world had struck. And what this meant was that slowly, gradually, but very *really*, the ancient heart of phogeydom – with all that it stood for, the instinctive and proper distrust of the new, the smart, the transformational, the glossy – was at risk. Only a few years before, the British had had a deep censorious wisdom that told them that, for example, it was funny to see Americans in brightly-coloured shirts, or in underpants that did not reach even down to their knees. Now, unquestionably, they were wearing them.

Of course, everywhere we went, we were told that the change was superficial, irrelevant, and would shortly go away. It was equally clear to us that such opinions, while reassuring to the phogey in all of us, were entirely wrong. The truth was that, as Britain jumped, feet foremost, into the great morass of the 1960s, it was only just entering the real testing time. The new order of society, the new shape of things, was just beginning to spread its tentacles everywhere, and they were in no sense absent from Britain. The new age – call it what one liked, the Age of Affluence, the Period of Participation, the Century of Consumerism – was here, and what is more it intended to stay. Even in Britain, then, the time of the Lonely Crowd, the Organization Man, and What the People Want was crossing the historical threshold. Most social observers of any merit were agreeing that there was a change, that the nation was becoming not what it was. The transition was hard to date: did one look to the death of Kipling, or the adventure of Suez, to the advent of the teenager, or of the cuffless trouser, or of commercial television for the great moment of transition? It was, equally, hard to define, and still is – though anyone who, like myself, has his pulse on the finger of contemporary society knows instinctively that it is there, feels it in his bones. Later we shall try not only to pinpoint some of the essential symptoms, but even to suggest some strategies and solutions to the crisis around us. But none of this will avail, unless we are quite clear what change it is that we are talking about. So let us first try to find a measure of what it is that has brought us to the moment at which we now stand.

*

There was indeed a time, and it is not at all remote, when the British were a traditional society, stable, hierarchical, and continuous. When they did things, they did them in much the way their fathers and grandfathers had always done them; and when they thought about the past, which they did often, a rosy glow came to their cheeks and a quiet pride shone in their eyes. The rich looked back on the great days of wealth; the poor, in the same spirit, looked back on the great days of poverty ('Oh, we was poor in them days,' they could always be found saying, 'All we had for supper was faggots and peas, and, when times was really bad, faggot and pea. But they were good days all the same, because people knew how to live then'). And how to live was indeed what people knew. They honoured their fathers, old swine though they might be, they loved their mothers, and they endeavoured to resemble both as much as was humanly possible. They fancied their past and preserved things from it, cultural things that they venerated the more as the patina of age grew on them; they found guidance in custom, and strength in old authority. They planted trees for their grand-children, and when they thought about the future, which they did from time to time, they saw it as a scrubbed version of the present.

Their houses were solid, their morals sturdy, their institutions substantial. And they themselves were solid in opinion, consistent in emotion, and they knew that they existed even when there was no one else in the room. They felt responsible for the quality of their own lives, and were so sure of their standards that they constantly imposed them on other people, even if this made them very miserable indeed. Though change existed, even in those days, they contrived to ignore it; and though strange yearnings might on occasion seize them, they used stiff-backed horsehair chairs and sofas, and endless cold baths, to make all discomforts seem external, and nothing to do with the psyche whatsoever. They were opposed to indulgence, sceptical of novelty, distrustful of fancy and desire. Sigmund Freud may have been needed in the erotic cosmopolitan hothouse of Vienna; he certainly had nothing at all to say to chilly

Cheam. Karl Marx may have got the problems of German capitalism right but as far as the British were concerned they knew exactly where to place him, which was in Highgate cemetery. For they distrusted politics in general, and considered they came from abroad. Equally, they distrusted abroad, and if necessary they colonized it frequently, in order to try to make it as English as possible.

In short, they knew exactly *who* they were and *what* they were and *why* they were. They believed in themselves and wanted themselves to endure, and they wanted everyone else to be exactly like them, knowing that there was nothing better to be. They were convinced of their own right-thinking and, when things went wrong, they blamed fate entirely, society very little, and their own unconscious motivations not at all. Their traditional skill was to give the anarchic world an appearance of order, an air of persistence and continuity. There was a hardy look in the national eye, a scepticism that always understood that the game, whatever it was, was not worth the candle. Whenever anything new was suggested, the native response was to say, first, that it couldn't be done and, second, that if it were it would all end in tears anyway. And the reason for this was simple and sensible; they were quite satisfied with life and with themselves as both already were. Nonetheless, under duress, they consented to lead the world; they flirted with exploration, industrial revolution, and colonization; they even allowed themselves to be somewhat modern. But they did this not for any of the lesser reasons sometimes attributed to them, and certainly not because they believed in change or transformation for their own sakes, but rather to keep this sort of activity in the right hands, since modernity was all too clearly the sort of thing that could easily be misused, and if they didn't do it someone else would, badly and wrongly. They went in for rapid industrial expansion in the nineteenth century, as any country that was the centre of the world obviously had to; but they did it as amateurs, members of a pastoral, traditional race playing at innovation, and they were not at all sorry to hand it over to others.

Sturdy, moralistic, law-abiding, inner-directed, and above all *always* right, they survived into the present when things began to change. For that present, when it turned up, proved to be a funny sort of present, not at all the sort of present a chap would choose if he had the choice. The old folk-wisdom, the stock of handed-down experience, no longer seemed quite to fit the case; change became so rapid, and events flickered by so fast, that people of one generation could understand nothing of the generation ten years older. This was not change as the British understood it; and worse things still were all part of it. For the world now seemed to be turning international, and no one took national pasts seriously any more. The authority enshrined in law, tradition, and moral codes no longer operated with the same precision. Indeed the old inner censors that had guided men for generations now stopped working; relativism came in, variousness was recognized, and instead of the view that God was English there grew up the view that man was international. People stopped having tradition, and when they thought of the past they groaned; it was only when they thought of the present, which they did all the time, that the rosy glow came into their cheeks and the pride to their eyes. Instead of tradition, they had fashion instead, and they began to buy their rôles and clothes, their psyches and their goods in all the newest stores. Something was evidently going wrong.

Indeed it appeared that the old world was beginning to go. Morals went out and sociology and psychology came in. Men were no longer right or wrong, good or bad, but socialized or deviant, adjusted or alienated; not only that, but deviance became the only valid form of socialization. Conscience was replaced by pure behaviour, emulation by ego, tradition by trauma, ancestors by angst. Psychic and social tensions grew; love and squalor could no longer be reconciled; the world seemed to be full of systems, explanations, religions and laws, no one of them righter than any

125

other. The old definitions of self quite disappeared; people no longer identified themselves by class, sex or rôle, anyone could do anything, and no one knew who he or she was any more, except when he, or perhaps she, reminded him- or herself by voting, or choosing one brand of detergent over another, or in one way or another managed to define themselves in the terms offered by the changed order of society. Thus, under this new order of things, people no longer knew *who* they were or *what* they were or *why* they were; instead they knew *that* they were, and found this fact very interesting. The desire to start from one's own existence and discover a world that fitted it became a great modern necessity; and these people were convinced of nothing and when things went wrong they blamed society in the first place and their own unconscious motivations in the second.

Naturally it was the Americans and the French who picked up on this sort of situation first; today, however, as we have already suggested, it has come to affect even the British. For a long time, with characteristic natural phlegm, they contrived to ignore the trend, but is has become quite clear that even in Britain we live in a world of flux, a society of anarchy, a universe in which what was true yesterday will no longer be true tomorrow. And these were the signs and symptoms that were all too visible as I came home from the United States. The great late twentieth-century lassitude was taking over. People would not go into pubs unless senseless mood music was playing on tapes in the background. Folk were watching *Match of the Day* on television instead of going out in their woolly mittens to watch the real thing. There were houses where central heating was being installed. People were putting things in the dustbin and throwing them away. Could it be, then, that England was changing for good, crossing over into that land from which no traveller ever returns? I examined all the signals – loss of grand convictions, desire not to be what one once had been, uncertainty about who the hell to be next, headaches, lassitude, tremors – and wisdom and experience led me to asseverate, quite firmly, *yes*. The past I had come back to was already in hiding, confined to the places where the television signal had not yet reached and the new boom economy not yet struck. And the change had come, not from the Conservative Party, not from the Labour Party, not even from the Liberal Party, but from the most powerful of all modern political forces, the remorseless global progress of mass consumer society.

Already it seemed that, were it not for the existence of foreigners with high expectations, the British, or many of them, were already quite forgetting just what they were supposed to be like. Happily, in the advertisements of transatlantic magazines like the *New Yorker*, there were images to help them – 'Come to Britain' publicity displaying happy images of thatched-roofed pubs in front of which sit, on benches, besmocked and thatched-roofed peasants; portraits of a blazered, bearded and patch-eyed gentleman who is gaily holding a horse in one hand and a bottle of tonic water in the other, over the legend 'Commander Whitehead is not eccentric, he is merely English'. It was thus that one was reminded of the land one was really presumed to live in: a pastoral, traditional land, its well-hedged fields filled with sheep, its small neat houses filled with class; a country rich in ivied walls, ancient castles, hollyhock-packed gardens, endless Coronations, Jubilees, and Changings of the Guard. Now the tourists came, peeking out of their air-conditioned buses, trying to catch a besmocked peasant or two on the fleeting lenses of their Polaroid land cameras; the odd besmocked peasant, the old umbrella-rolled and pinstripe-suited city gent, did emerge fleetingly, only to dash into the nearest supermarket to buy a TV lunch or get home to watch the American quiz-shows on television.

The phogey may struggle gamely on, ignoring and pooh-poohing: not a bad idea, in the end. But the shift is inevitable. What to call it, how to describe it? Americanization, some people say, but this is hardly accurate. It is a global process; and a better name, the one we have already suggested, is *-ization*, which is going on everywhere and making everywhere like everywhere else. Indeed change everywhere is *-ization*'s business, and its main reward or promise is to suggest that change was exactly what we've all been needing for a long time, having had too much of the same. So the culture of *-ization* is unnational, untraditional, polyglot, parodic: it is everything that phogey is not. Its aim is not to help you remember who you are but make you forget it; it swamps, seduces and lures, the sort of thing phogeys would never do under any circumstances. And once your old identity is forgotten it is prompt in offering you a new one: the answer is *Consumo ergo sum*. What fills the gaps in life it has so carefully created is, precisely, its own commodities, which are not just goods, but ways of being, identities, memberships. Like all change, one of its qualities is its fleetingness, and this makes it very hard to characterize. Nonetheless, I will now proceed to do so.

PART SIX

HOW TO
BE A
NUMBER
FOR THE
IBM

This book deals with two worlds, two orders of society. What, then, is the difference between them? The following alphabet explains.

(*a*) In traditional societies, goods that are brought in from other lands are labelled FOREIGN. Everyone knew what this meant: that they were unreliable, came from some dark place or other you could not possibly trust, and were quite inferior to anything whatsoever that had been made at home. In the consumer society such goods are now labelled IMPORTED, and this is honorific. It means that they are by nature far more interesting than anything made at home, that they have the patina of abroad on them – the glow of foreign holidays in the sun, of iced drinks and crisp ski-slopes, of dark oriental passages where, in an opium haze, small yellow men make advanced electrical goods of a sophistication impossible to conceive of here. Now it is BRITISH MADE that is the warning, meaning that things come from some dark place or other where production interrupts tea-breaks and not the other way round, and is naturally quite inferior to anything from Abroad. This is why the goods made in Birmingham or Stepney have to have *Italian-styled* or *American-type* written all over them, in order that they can imbibe just enough foreignness actually to sell them.

(*b*) In traditional societies, it is always necessary to suggest that goods have been made in exactly the same way for a very long time, because this means they have been tried and tested, finished and perfected. In consumer societies, this means that they are unstyled and simply out of date, unless they have been around so long that they can come back again as bygones. Ideally, in the consumer society, no one object should stay the same for more than about three months; it must be IMPROVED or RESTYLED and be given a new product number: the XCW3542c, suggesting it is one of a long chain of versions of which there will be many many more. By the same token, in traditional societies, again to give goods the appearance of permanence, it was often emphasized that they were 'Home-Made', or had royal or aristocratic associations. ('Made according to the recipe of a Nobleman in the County of Worcester,' older hands will remember reading on bottles of Worcestershire sauce.) Now home-made simply means that things are not even properly wrapped up, and the aristocratic association means that the goods are doubtless over-priced and certainly primarily intended for foreign tourists, perhaps in duty-free airport shops. Today the only worthwhile patrons of any goods are the trendiest of pop stars; their be-drugged and drunken approval of anything is universally read as an act of critical cunning as shrewd as a Bernard Berenson attribution of a painting to Titian.

(c) In traditional societies, the social function of a human being is to produce. People exist to provide labour, or brains, or brawn, to make, lift, dig, push, think, tug, invent. For this they are paid certain sums of money, and invited to save them: the appropriate mottoes are *Time is money*, *Earn all you can*, *Dig for Victory*, *A penny saved is a penny gained*. In consumer societies, of course, the social function of a human being is not to produce – we have machines to do that – but, of course, to consume. For existing, people are paid sums of money; and they are invited to spend it. Indeed, in a consumer society, consuming is the real work, work so demanding that it invades all our leisure time as well. The appropriate mottoes are *Relax and let X take the strain*, *Spoil yourself with a Y*, and *Go to bed with a Z*. Conscientiousness may have gone from production; it is found in full measure in consumption. Indeed most of our free time is spent in thinking about, or watching, or reading about consuming, even when we are not actually doing it; and anyone who neglects this is committing a contemporary crime, that of failing to keep the economy buoyant.

(*d*) Likewise, in traditional societies people believe that thriftiness is virtue. They love possessions and think it is wrong to throw something out, even if it is broken or was only wrapped round or contained or tied up something.* In consumer societies, if you drop something on the floor, you naturally toss it away, because everything is disposable, non-returnable, or throwaway, and everything is by definition obsolete the moment you have bought it.

(*e*) In traditional societies, people believe in privacy, live behind drawn curtains, and believe that, if you have a home or a family, there is no need for neighbours or friends at all. Indeed it is assumed that the natural condition of a person is solitary, a person being most a person when entirely alone. In consumer societies, it is assumed that the natural condition of a person is communal, and that non-existence occurs when one is excluded from a group. In contemporary America, everything is now done in groups. You date in groups, you grade students in groups, you think in groups, at bull-sessions or conferences, and you even create art in groups. (This is why the two main art-forms of the consumer society are the film and the musical, for both are created by committees.) Privacy is unpleasant, publicity is all. The natural product of the consumer society is the picture window – a device invented, of course, not that people might the better see out, but that other people might the better see in. The consumer society is one in which it is a socially aggressive act to draw one's curtains at night. It suggests that one might have something to hide, and in this post-Freudian age it is not hard to guess what; but, worse, it

* In New England – America's one vestigially traditional society, apart, of course from some parts of the South – the thrifty citizens are said to keep two boxes in their homes: one for used pieces of string to use again, the other for string too short to be saved.

suggests one might have *nothing* to hide, or to show either, nothing to display, no rich friends, well-dressed mistresses, or fashionable company, no art, no books or bibelots, no tan. In America no one ever believes that anyone wishes to be private; indeed the desire can only display trauma, personality-impediment, incapacity to adjust to the group. It is not surprising that the latest thing in the States is the all-glass elevator and the all-glass house, at which nobody should throw stones. In the all-glass house there is one walled room, in the centre, for the one purpose still regarded, in some quarters at least, as private; but people can watch you going into that and keep track of how long you stay.

(*f*) In pre-consumer societies, your milk is brought to your door by a friendly milkman. In consumer societies, your milk, if delivered at all, and not simply made available at the supermarket, is brought to your door, if he remembers, by a hateful milkman, who drops bottles on the step and doesn't clean up, rings the doorbell while you are in the lavatory, whistles at your daughter, and so on. With the milk he leaves notes, written by public relations experts at the Milk Fobbing Council. These notes attempt to blackmail you into buying more milk by explaining that everywhere cows are bursting, milkmen being laid off, and society being put at risk because you can only manage to digest a lousy two pints of the stuff a day. These notes are always signed: 'Your friendly milkman.'

(*g*) In traditional societies, there are artists, and if they are good at their task they are held in a certain esteem by society. These artists are persons who, having worked hard in the classical stuff of their craft, having disciplined themselves carefully and studied the history and aesthetics of their medium, have now at last submitted themselves to the public's praise or blame. The public's judgment on them is roughly the judgment of other professionals; the best singers are those who have trained longest, know most about their art, and are the nicest, most intelligent, most charming people. In consumer societies, there are non-artists, and they are held in high esteem by society. In such societies, talent is an accidental attribute; artists are just anybody and once they have been described as such they are allowed to get away with anything. The public's judgment on them is administered not by other professionals but by journalists; and the best singers are those who cannot sing, who know nothing about music, but have the best contracts and the best agents. Likewise, whereas in the traditional society the great writers were those who knew the most and saw most deeply, today the great writers are those who appear on television most often to talk about 'me art', write about the most fashionable dilemmas and seem most like 'one of us'. The point is that in the consumer society artists are not so much prophets as models; they prove to us all that we each may, without doing any real work, be discovered, become rich, and make the big time.

(*h*) In consumer societies, nothing costs as much as it is supposed to, except when it costs more (law). In such societies everything is a special offer, or has threepence off, or is free with something else. The only exceptions are things which are marked with prices *excl. purchase tax* or *first payment*, and these of course cost more.

(*i*) Think of advertising as it was and is now. Once advertisements, dignified and sober, politely drew your honour's attention to 'The Original Celebrated CURIOUSLY STRONG PEPPERMINTS. Medicinal lozenges. "ALTOIDS" AID DIGESTION. From Chemists Only.'* Today it is 'GOT THE SPANGLES?' (A hypochondriacal aunt of mine ran off to the doctor when this advertisement appeared: 'I really think I have got them,' she told him). Or it is a television commercial, showing our modern folk-heroes, that young† couple in

---

* And weren't there some lozenges advertised as being used by Sarah Bernhardt and two eminent dukes?
† In traditional societies, folk-heroes are always old, because wisdom is valued; in consumer societies, folk-heroes are always young, because innocence is valued – innocent people spend more.

their fisherman's-knit sweaters who are the model of all we seek to be, jigging frenetically about and chanting 'Pop 'em in, suck 'em down, Make you dance all round the town (Mmm! Delicious!)' Or compare the advertisements for James Braithwaite, Ltd. The old advertisement showed James standing, proud and rotund, outside his factory, a thing he always had plenty of time to do. The new advertisements show the rear-lights of a car disappearing through the Mersey Tunnel; the caption reads 'Today, Manchester for COTTON TALKS! Tomorrow, Ceylon for TEA TALKS! Wednesday, Wall Street for MONEY TALKS! The J. B. of today is RAISING THE STANDARD OF LIFE – FOR YOU!'

(*j*) In the traditional society, the function of transport is to convey persons between two places inconveniently apart. In the consumer society, the function of transport is to consume petrol and car and road. Once people went to the pub round the corner; now they go to a pub fifteen miles out into the country, in order to stretch their legs – on the accelerator and clutch – going to and fro. Likewise the great vogue for car-rallies, which are simply a means of using your car to the full before it depreciates.

(*k*) In the consumer society, articles which are used for doing something nice are sold as if they themselves were nice. Thus, though it is in fact the programmes that are (sometimes) exciting, the advertisements contrive to suggest that it is the sets themselves which are. In this way mechanisms for doing things can actually become indispensible even though they are never used, and there are people who never watch television but are unable to manage without a set.

(*l*) In traditional societies it is the men who work, while women are centred in the home. In consumer societies, women are encouraged to go out to work, and by labouring they are thus able to earn money to buy labour-saving devices for the home they are rarely in. The reason for this is not so much that the society needs female labour as that it needs female spending.

(*m*) In a pre-consumer society, the word *new* is rarely honorific – it is more often than not pejorative. To say, in such societies, that something is second-hand means that it has the patina of age upon it, and therefore is probably better. In consumer societies, everything is labelled NEW! NEW! NEW!, even when it isn't. In due course, however, the wheel comes full circle; modern goods prove so shoddy that people start to buy old things because they are properly made. Hence the sign I saw in America: 'New! New! Antiques!' This will soon happen here.

(*n*) In the traditional society, art is solid, moralistic and public and everyone can understand it, while artists are treated with general respect. In the consumer society, art – not being what the public want, being a selective product – becomes anarchistic, alienated and difficult, and no one can understand it at all, while artists are treated with general contempt. On the other hand, the producers of sub- or mass-art are public heroes.

(*o*) In consumer societies, whenever you buy anything, you need something else to go with it. Thus one buys a camera and discovers one needs a strap and a viewfinder and a picture-projector and a screen; one buys a car and discovers one needs windscreen washers and foglamps and demisters and little round chrome portholes to put on the bonnet. Many of these additional objects are to make mass-produced things appear individual; except that the objects are themselves mass-produced.

(*p*) In consumer societies, the marginal is always inflated into the necessary. Television sets are marginal; central heating is marginal; cars are marginal – they are fripperies on the edge of life. Just recently in America it has become accepted that two bathrooms are necessary, perhaps because the consumer society is highly productive of dirt, perhaps because it is also highly productive of protection against the things it produces. This trend toward a larger number of necessities means that the notion of what constitutes poverty changes; and it makes difficulties for snobs, who depend for their ostentation on possessing marginal things.

(*q*) In consumer societies, the drift of the economy is toward finding ways of selling nothing. The nearest thing that has so far been developed in this search has been the nylon stocking, the manufacturers of which, in a pre-consumer society, would be prosecuted for fraud. Beautifully packed, with excellent newpaper, television and point-of-sale advertising, placed in an eye-catching position on a supermarket shelf, Nothing will doubtless soon be on the market. The only trouble is that it requires no plant and no labour to make, and will therefore not keep the economy buoyant enough; therefore research – which also keeps the economy buoyant and makes the universities viable – is currently trying to find a way of making Nothing out of something.

(*r*) In traditional societies, schools are bare, harsh, strict places with hard benches and stern teachers, and their teaching is centred round abstracts – manners, morals, social ideals. In consumer societies, schools are comfortable, homely, friendly places with soft seats and amiable teachers, and their teaching is centred around apparatus. Further, in non-consumer societies, schools are local, and their purpose is to fit people to live in the neighbourhood. In the consumer society, schools are centralized, and their purpose is to fit people to live anywhere the consumer society chooses to send them. This leads us to

(*s*) In traditional societies, people live where they used to and feel ties of kinship and affection to their unit of society, which is small and therefore well-known. In the consumer society you can live anywhere because it is just like the place you just left. Everywhere has the same chain-stores, the same goods, the same shop-fronts in the same global architectural style. People are embarrassed to live in villages without concrete lamp-standards, or towns with old buildings; thus Shrewsbury town council is waging a campaign against the mediaeval look of the town, which is the only thing that stops it from being Slough. Anyone who doubts the new trend should visit the rebuilt centre of Southampton. The shops are built in uniform contemporary and the stores that occupy them all come from somewhere else, because they are the only organizations which can afford the high rents that such modern properties command. Anything that was regional, local and small has disappeared; and Southampton is just Anywhere. In short, it doesn't exist.

(*t*) In consumer societies, people do not know their identities, and are trying to find them; in traditional societies, people know theirs all too well, and are trying to lose them. 'Who is any of us?' wrote a friend of mine, in a satire of American Shakespeare criticism. And American Shakespeare criticism, with its insistence on the problem of identity, defines not Shakespeare, but the modern world: who, indeed, *is* any of us?

(*u*) In traditional societies, at Christmas, people have Christmas trees and send out cards wishing you well for the New Year. In the consumer society, at Christmas, it is factories and offices and businesses that have Christmas trees and fairy lights and banners wishing you the best of the season with their compliments. During the year the same factories and offices put advertisements in the paper saying A LITTLE LEARNING IS A DANGEROUS THING (A. Pope) or MEN OF DISTINCTION PREFER GOD. This is called non-advertising or public relations. It is simply conspicuous consumption by corporations instead of people and what it means, in effect, is YOU PEOPLE OUT THERE ARE JUST CRUMBS AND WE COULD BUY EVERY ONE OF YOU UP IF WE WISHED.

(*v*) Consumer societies do not like people with odd tastes. I happen to like steaks extremely rare, almost uncooked. However when I go into an English restaurant I am always – in spite of my caveats – brought well-done steak, usually described to me by the waiter as 'ever so rare, sir'. On one occasion when I protested that words were not the same as deeds, I was told by the waiter; 'I'm sorry sir, we can't do them rare; people don't like them.' What people – a lot of people – don't like is *out*.

(*w*) In traditional societies, when you have bought something, you feel a sense of well-being which continues as long as you keep the object. In consumer societies, your desire for the object diminishes the moment you have left the shop; and by the time you get home you are radically dissatisfied and want an improved model.

(*x*) In a traditional society goods are sold unwrapped and unnamed and this is because you are interested in the goods themselves; but in the consumer society the competition between goods is not for the best product but for the best pack. It is in fact entirely the wrapping which sells things; hence the appearance of sober books in wicked covers.

(*y*) In consumer societies, people are always trying to invent ways of spending the money they have. If you have a car, you must buy a boat; if you have a boat, then you must go in for an aeroplane. The result is that you use more and more things less and less. However, you must find room for them, clean them, service them and finance their depreciation. To have so much is like having nothing, except that you can't get away from it.

(*z*) In the traditional society, people felt that they existed on earth to enrich it, to make it a better place, to build things for its future, to add to its stock of ideas and institutions. In the consumer society, however, it is assumed that man is a wastrel – a creature put on this earth in order to destroy goods, so that they have to be replaced. His human service is to take what is new and pristine and to make it worth less than it was before. In the traditional society, people build standards to endure and houses to last. In the consumer society, houses are built to fall to pieces, and there are no standards but simply fashions.

The consumer society does, you see, have a real zest for experience. What it believes, to put the matter in a word, is that you can never have too much of a good thing. It is nothing if not expansive. A friend of mine came up to me the other day after reading all the plans and pleas for commercial radio and said rather gloomily: 'Why do we always have to have *more*? Why can't we have a campaign for *less* of everything?' The truth of the matter is that the desire to have less of what we have and nothing at all of what we haven't is, in the present situation, quite anarchic. The time will come when those of us who choose not to have things will be made to pay for not having them – just as in American juke-boxes silence is already a purchaseable commodity. Once the world was full of it, free. The same is true of the space where you leave cars. Once the world was rich in space; now one has to pay rental in order to pause for a moment in a public street. The consumer society gradually comes to the point where everything people once took for granted has to be consciously chosen; and, as is characteristic in this world, what is chosen has to be paid for. This is called consumer existentialism, and is much more important than the other kind.

PART SEVEN

CHOICES, CHOICES ALL THE TIME

There it is, then: pinned and transfixed, mapped and charted, the force of change that is subtly eroding the old phogey world, and bringing even to Britain the crudest of human urges, the desire for membership of the present. The old society of self-help is disappearing, and the new society of self-service is taking its place. But what, you are now asking, does this mean for me? A good deal, I'm afraid. For, whatever the phogey says, we will not be allowed to continue as we have done. The new order of things demands nothing less than a new morality, indeed a new kind of human being. It has its new ethics, its new priesthood, its new ways of conducting a life. Later in this book, some tactics of avoidance will be suggested; at this stage, it is well to know what will be demanded of us.

Not too long ago, in the United States, a Dr Ernest Dichter, who, as a motivation research expert is recognizably one of the new high priests of the new order of things, put his finger on one of the essential problems of the time. The problem, he said, was one at the heart of the ethical life itself. For what now had to be done was nothing less than to transpose the modern individual from his old work-ethic to the new fun-ethic, for we had to make it quite clear to people that they are being moral when they are spending, flirting, wife-swapping, driving two cars at once, or taking three vacations a year. Indeed, in the new sort of society, such things are the most important things they do, our main social duties being not as producers but as consumers. Therefore it is necessary to reinstate hedonism, an ethic which unfortunately has not been too popular for centuries, ever since the Puritans put on their pointed hats and started to shake the moral finger at people, but has now become an economic necessity. Enjoyment is not an easy thing to have, but now that it has become socially necessary people must be persuaded that it is not too bad a thing to go in for at all. And the best way to do this, Dr Dichter explained, was to make it quite clear that hedonism is normal, by showing people images of other people enjoying themselves, and getting away with it everywhere in public. In one sense, Dr Dichter had to admit, this was not morality at all – morality being, after all, the pleasure that you feel from *not* doing what you always wanted to do. But what the new society had to do was abolish *morality* and substitute for it *behaviour*. Thus, instead of the Ten Commandments, we need the Ten Statistics; instead of *Pilgrim's Progress*, we need the *Kinsey Report*, a book designed to allow people to inspect the sexual behaviour of others and check on whether they are doing it properly themselves.

Today it is growingly by behaviour that we live. In the traditional society, the crucial figure was the priest, who judged conduct. In the new society, the crucial figure is the sociologist, who reports on it, or the psychologist, who observes that all social abrasions and psychological tensions are simply caused by lack of adjustment. At the same time it has to be recognized that behaviour is not all that easy, and that a good deal of effort has to be put into making people do it. There was, for example, a time when people didn't know what they wanted. If you were poor, there was not much point in wanting anything anyway, since if you did you couldn't have it; if you were rich, there was no reason at all to want anything either, since you already had it. Now, however, we live in the time of What the People Want; the only difficulty is to make sure that they actually do want it, and much of modern culture is devoted to this end. For it is only if people want a thing that it can be made; or, rather, if a thing is to be made, it has to be ensured that people want it. And, while it is true that everywhere you go people do seem to want things, they often do not want the right things, or want them badly enough, or often enough, or at the right time, to keep the economy working. People have to keep on wanting what there is, but, even more importantly, if the economy is to grow, they have to keep on wanting what there *isn't*: the thing that is to come next, the item that is to replace and make obsolete the one they have just this minute acquired.

Thus a new kind of human being, a creature of desire and discontent, quite unlike the old phogey, has to be generated: the sort of person who hates what they have, uses what they don't need, and dreams of what does not even exist yet. Let us look in more detail at some of the ways in which this works. For example: for years the tobacco industry has been looking in fury at that vast audience of persons who, when offered a cigarette, that phallic and libidinous tube which distinguishes modern man (as a lady-friend of mine observed on looking at Da Vinci's *Last Supper*, on display, at three times the original size, at Forest Lawn Cemetery in California, 'Some supper, none of them are smoking'), 'I don't smoke.' How does one make them feel uncomfortable and mean? How, more importantly, does one provide them with some sort of non-cigarette that lets them appear to smoke without doing so? Early, naïve attempts were made to deal with the problem: the metholated cigarette, for people who wanted to feel that, while they were contracting lung-cancer, they were also getting rid of bronchial catarrh; the chocolate-flavoured cigarette, for those who wanted to smoke and eat chocolate at the same time; the filter-tipped cigarette, or the cigarette with the condom; and so on. But now newer techniques have been invented, fiendish in their subtlety; and an American brand called Tareyton has come up with what is probably the definitive answer to the problem. The brand has two filters, one black and one white; the advertisements show a man cutting open the cigarette to expose the filters, remarking: 'There's a lot of satisfaction in pointing out something good to a friend.

That's why it often happens that one cigarette out of a pack of Dual Filter Tareyton never does get smoked. People break it open to demonstrate its unique Dual Filter containing Activated Charcoal.

Yes, well, what, you may say; but one step more, and we are there. For here is one of those intellectual breakthroughs that revolutionize merchandising. It says, simply, that there are other things you can do with cigarettes beside smoking them – things like breaking them open, cutting them in half, tearing off the paper and scattering the contents over steak, etc. In short, the manufacturers have found a true product, a producty sort of product, one that has something for everyone, even those who do not like it at all. A small illustration, yes; but it contains a large truth. For it reminds us that in this world there are many things that exist, and yet they do not, *really*; this is because they have not yet been *marketed*. If they have not been marketed, they do not have a definition, an image, a shimmer of implication and possibility; they function, as Jean-Paul Sartre would say – if he ever bothered about this sort of thing, instead of worrying so much about being *en soi* – in a void of non-being. On the other hand, with good marketing, with a patina of imagery, it is possible to sell anything, or even nothing, just as long as it has the *right associations*. There was a time, in the old world, the phogey world, when things were just that, things. A car was a car, and not your mistress or your best advertisement; a book was a thing to read, and not proof that you were cultured, informed, or had a coffee table to put it on; a newspaper was likewise a throwaway printed text containing facts, and not evidence that you were a top person or had a lively mind. But things are no longer enough as things; they now have to be incorporated into life-style, adjusted to the psyche, and the psyche, in turn, adjusted to them, in a happy symbiosis.

Let me turn again to my American experience, as I will do for much of what follows. There is a reason for this; of all modern societies, America exemplifies the dominant new

mode of discourse, which is phatic communion. We have
had occasion to use this concept before; but it is, you will
recall, speech that seeks to share feelings rather than actually to communicate, as lovers and babies do. As a result of my
American voyages, I have begun to develop a small and still
provisional concept of how this works, which I call HAVERN-
IZATION. I was led to this notion when, flying, as one can
now, across the Atlantic, we reached our destination,
crowded the aisles, hitting each other with briefcases in
order to get off first, met the sagging array of stewardesses
by the door, their ankles swollen, their speech virtually
gone, and one of them offered the ravaged rictus of an
over-used smile toward me, and murmured: 'Come back
again, and havernize day.' Throughout America, I then
noticed, this same formula was used repeatedly in all possible situations: '(I, we) hope you enjoyed your (meal, room,
flight, conversation with me, love-affair with me) and
havernize (day, evening, weekend, drink, marriage,
divorce).' The nouns are irrelevant, the function being
the phatic one of casting a sacramental glow over whatever is happening, the dull banality of the real, time itself.

There are, of course, many variants. After serving you a
notably poor meal, your waitress will come by the table to
invest the occasion with magic: 'Isn't it wonderful here?'
she'll say. In the motel room, the questionnaire left on the
dressing table, asking you to compliment the management,
inquires: 'Maybe this wasn't the most fantastic experience
of your whole life, but it came close, right?' Yet steak and
room feel better after the words have surrounded them,
making it clear that in the modern world the word has an
important function – not to describe reality, but to invent it.
Hence 'Havernization' – and it is becoming world-wide
(with the possible exception of Russia). Menus everywhere
now describe their food in detail, naming every steak as
'succulent', every sauce as 'piquant', every wine as 'full',
until the meal itself, when it comes, can only be a drab

approximation to the verbal fiction.* At the same time, we ourselves become verbal fictions too, articulating ourselves in much the same language. And it is this new patina-ed world that we have to understand, if we are to know what is threatening the phogey in us. Let us now inspect it in a little more detail, examining some of the primary mechanisms of its operation:

1. GOVERNMENT BY HAVERNIZATION

One of the most important things about traditional societies is that nothing new ever happens in them, and if it should happen then no one ever needs to know about it, since it is assumed that it has always happened somewhere else before anyway. Therefore in such societies there is no such thing as publicity, there is no news, there is indeed no novelty. Because there is no news, literacy is quite unimportant, since anything that matters can be shouted into the next human ear; word of mouth, invasion beacons, and the striking of church clocks can perform all the acts of transmission necessary. This is the great difference between the old order and the new, for in the new order acts of language and communication are of dominant importance.

In consumer societies, then, people believe that every-thing that is happening, to them or anyone else, is actually

* Yes, descriptions do make things seem different. I had a basket the other day that came with this tag:
'With warm wishes of the thoughtful friend, whose name appears on the outer carton, who sent 'way out here to Oregon, for something mighty fine . . . just for you this *Fruit Buffet*.
'Delightful and exciting things have happened in the con-fectionizing of this wonderful fruit. For instance, those 'Apricot Sandwiches'. Eat them like a sandwich – it's great! And those Calimyra figs – Oh boy! Fact is, every piece in the box is something you might find on a dreamer's holiday, at the end of a rainbow or somewhere west of the moon.
'Harry and David at Bear Creek Orchards, out Medford, Oregon, way.'
It was funny; it didn't taste like fruit, after that.

happening for the first time. And, because everything is so new, so novel, so demanding of everyone else's attention, these things have to be imaged, refracted, eternalized. They have to be reported to the newspapers. They have to be filmed. They have to be tape-recorded. They have to be photographed. And the point is that if these things are not done, then the event doesn't count; a thing which only happens once, quietly, doesn't exist. Thus there are in the modern world persons who no longer go away on holiday to enjoy themselves; they go simply to take photographs. They then show themselves the photographs; and so have their holiday in the sitting room, at home, afterwards. I once asked an American whether he had ever been to Europe: 'I went this summer,' he said, 'but I don't remember anything about it, because I haven't had time to look at my slides yet.' And, similarly, in consumer societies people believe that anything that happens in private doesn't exist. Thus diplomatic meetings behind closed doors are considered not secret but non-existent; and they have to be repeated in public before people will believe in them at all.

Thus traditional societies believe in privacy, whereas the consumer society believes in publicity. Likewise, traditional societies are interested in standards, while the consumer society is interested in events. Knowing things has a rare thrill for the consumer society; it believes that people have a *right* to know, even when they are not in the least interested. The mass-medium is its great instrument of knowing, and its attitude toward things, like the sociologists', is permissive – it is interested in events because they happen, and people because they are newsworthy, and not because either are good or bad. In consumer societies news is concerned with the marginal, the deviant, and the exceptional; and it ignores the necessary and the ordinary, which become increasingly old-hat and unfashionable. Novelty pleases for its own sake. Publicity becomes a value in itself, independent of what the publicity is for; the Sunday press is constantly approached by people who want to be exposed, and television programmes are packed with folk who are only too happy to be shown as ridiculous and absurd, provided that they are shown. In this way, the press not only describes news but also makes it, because it decides what constitutes news. What it chooses to tell us is automatically what we find we want to know.

Newspapers in fact create a climate of news; they now plan what size they will be long before they know what events will occur, and if not enough do occur they will make some.* Since there has to be news, this opens the way for sensation seekers (be they flagpole squatters or protest marchers) and public relations men, who want to be in it. Many of the events described by the papers are specially created for them; if they didn't exist, the events wouldn't. Thus little ever happens on a Saturday – wars are not allowed to start and crimes are not allowed to be committed – because the weekend is a bad news time. In fact, there are wars – like the one in Katanga – which are simply presented for the pressmen – and if they went away the war would stop. Indeed, one can't help suspecting that if one abolished the press one would abolish wars as well – and certainly there would be less crime, less protest, less fashionable behaviour, and less goings on among the smart set. The beat generation would not exist – it was the press who, finding this brand of bohemianism newsworthy, wrote articles about it and showed photographs of beats being sick in California motels; and so enabled every university campus in America to become populated with outsiders overnight. Or consider juvenile delinquency; the way juvenile delinquency works is that young people read about what delinquents in other areas are doing, and then do it. In this way news is self-sustaining; it provides a model for others – and so produces more news.

* News of course, expands to fit the place available for it; thus, during the war, when newspapers were of four pages, one never felt that one was being deprived of news, even though there was so much more of it about.

Thus while in a traditional society no news is good news, in a consumer society no news would mean that people would cease to know how to behave. One of the main agencies for making it known what kind of behaviour and what kind of man is In this year is the mass-medium, which has taken over from religion and tradition as an agency of human guidance. Just as it helps delinquents find themselves, and know that delinquents is what they are, so for all of us it offers a model of conduct. Each of us can find out what sort of chap he is, and how he ought to act, what he ought to wear and what opinions he should express in order to act the kind of man he is to perfection. There was a time when newspapers, particularly the intellectual ones, used to encompass a liberal variety of opinions within their pages. Thus the *Observer* would represent the opinions of both left-wing and right-wing intellectuals, and allow that what mattered was not one's attitude toward Goa but the intelligence with which one held it. But this sort of approach has proved too schizoid; it affords a woolly brand image. And so now newspapers have a model reader – a particular kind of top person or lively mind, to whom the whole paper is directed; and the idea is that *you* should become *him* or *her*.

The mass-media, in short, tell us how life should be lived, what is in style now,* how we should keep our homes and gardens, and how far we should let our boyfriends go (the answer to this is, incidentally, a little further each year). Communications thus become so important to us, and become such an industry, that they must go on finding more and more hotter and hotter news, and a kind of hysterical process ensues by which so much is communicated so much of the time that we can scarcely hear what is said. I wasn't at

---

* 'In a woman's world, '61 was a swinging, fast-moving, pace-setting year. There was so much happening all the time it took a really "with it" girl to keep up,' said the *Daily Mirror* as the year turned, adding: 'Wake up there! . . . Learn to stop, look and listen before you shake your head . . . and remember that inside every square (we do mean you) there's a with-it girl trying to get out and have fun.'

all surprised to hear from an American friend the other day that a toothpaste had been evolved that actually was better than all other toothpastes, and that the manufacturers now found themselves quite unable to tell the public about it. All the interstices of communication were closed; all the brands of toothpaste had been crying wolf for so many years that the news simply couldn't break its way into the world; the vast shouting match had claimed this so many times that no one was now listening. The fact that my friend had heard about it, however, does provide a moment of cheer – small guerrilla bands of well-informed toothpaste users are roaming the country, with the light of truth in their eyes; and one is reassured to know that if a really important piece of news ever breaks in America – like a war, for instance – it stands some chance of breaking through the communications jam, and will probably be believed – after, of course, it has been tested and vetted by *Which?* or *Consumer Report.*

I must say, as a fairly regular visitor to America, that the first real intimation I get of the true feel of American life is the sense of being overly communicated to. As the ship goes in past Nantucket, and the wireless waves crackle and boom, the telegraph starts tapping, and the radar begins to spin, I know I'm getting there. Since I am by habit a congenital listener, a congenital watcher, a congenital reader, America is, to me, a perpetual assault. Billboards flagellate the eye, radios drum on the ear, television pummels me in the face; and everywhere there is something to read – from the flickering news bulletins given in lights on the Times building to the sign DIG WE MUST – FOR A GREATER NEW YORK on the road-mender's trestles.*

Indeed, there are times when I suspect that the only people who do *attend* to all this communication are the visitors, whose responses are pristine. Sometimes, in fact, I feel that I am the only person in America who ever reads or

---

* The strange thing is, they've been digging ever since I've been going there, and still they haven't found it.

hears things; mass communications have communicated so much, and public relations have related to the public so thoroughly, that American man now lies lethargic and entirely unmoved beneath the hail of news and views. And perhaps it is because the communicators realize this fact that their efforts are given with ever increasing frenzy. Information now has to be distributed at such a level of hysteria, to make the public listen, that it is frightening; and with each new breakthrough in hysteria the public listens the less.

I remember once meeting in New York an English friend of mine, a doctor, who had come to America only the day before. It was his first visit to the States, and he told me of a disturbing experience. He had stepped off the boat, taken a taxi to his hotel, and casually, while shaving, turned on the radio. It was not the sort of thing he would do at home, because he is not a casual man, but America tempts this sort of thing. For a moment, the radio lulled him with music; and then, suddenly, a voice intervened. 'Cancer,' it cried, 'is striking now. Are you eating less? Are your lips peeling? Do you notice swellings? Rush to a doctor now!' My friend snatched up his medical bag and ran down to the lobby. 'I'm a doctor!' he cried, 'Stay calm!' Then he noticed that calm was precisely what everyone else was; the scene of national disaster he imagined was nowhere in evidence; a few people in the lobby looked up apathetically at his behaviour, and, beyond the windows, normal crowds drifted past. Society was not disorganized; no one was a mite concerned. It was just that he listened to things.

He returned to his room, reflecting that in fact there was no reason why there was any more cancer on this day than on any other. The radio was still playing trauma music; and in the intervals the frantic voices would come on. He listened and realized that not only were they advertising goods; they were also advertising diseases, values, social roles. 'Hurry! Hurry! Run to the nearest drugstore and buy tissues. You may have a hole in your nose!' *'Turn on your faucet now!* Do you know it costs only a nickel to leave your faucet running for one hour? This advertisement was brought to you as a public service by the Water Corporation of your town.' 'Stop a teacher on the street and give him your wallet!' 'Pack up your home and send it now to Radio Free Asia!' 'Adopt a juvenile delinquent!' 'Take your worst enemy to church!' My friend prescribed himself a tranquillizer, the first he had ever taken, and sat down to wait for it to take effect. The radio fought back. 'Are you anxious, jittery, traumatized? Do you have an inexplicable feeling that your toes are loose? Take tranquillizers. Look – here are three similar tablets of different brands, and here is a perspex replica of your great intestine. Watch what product A does to it. See how it burns, irritates, destroys essential tissue . . .'

The consumer society does indeed have a gift for such tension-producing machines, because the only way to assuage yourself is to buy things. I remember being roused to much the same condition on my own first visit to America, when I took a trip across the country by car with an American friend. The traffic, the turnpikes, the speed quickly had me trembling, but what upset me the most were the traffic signs. When you drive in America, the eye is bombarded, not only by advertisements for motels and gas and Burmashave, not only by the names of towns, but by the informational signs that the government put up, which are of astounding frequency and impact. GO SLOW CHILDREN I could take; THICKLY SETTLED and ACCIDENT AREA heated me a little; WATCH FOR SNOW PLOWS worried me, since it was mid-summer. DEER CROSSING struck me as a trifle quaint, and SIGN AHEAD seemed a bit inbred – though typical of the news about news that the consumer society goes in for. HEAVY CROSS TRAFFIC was a bit worse, with its indication that trucks and buses were perpetually bursting out at speed from hidden defiles (but when you got there you saw nothing), while CONSTRUCTION – PROCEED AT YOUR OWN RISK meant, quite simply, don't proceed at all (but when you got there there were three men leaning on shovels). Gradually, however, a disturbing undertone began to grow, not only from the kind but the number of signs; gradually the note of menace was built up. BARRICADE AHEAD suggested revolutionary situations, and the signs that told you that the highway would be closed in the event of war were singularly nerve-racking, since one didn't know what the situation was since the last news broadcast. There were even signs which told you what kind of accident to have – AVOID REAR END COLLISIONS (preferring, no doubt, good old front end collisions) – and an accelerating note of menace that increased at every roadside (KENTUCKY MORTI-CIANS WELCOME FAST DRIVERS TO OUR STATE).

It is true that, in England, we have not yet reached the level of full assault by communication, but it is coming, as is all too clear when you go to a party these days and find that everyone there is from the media. Our traffic signs remain pitched in a spirit of low key pleading (saying, in effect, DO BE CAREFUL NOW, WON'T YOU? and SOMEWHAT BUSY JUNC-TION JUST ROUND THE CORNER) and our newspapers report the endless crises of life with only a small amount of hysteria. But it is on the way, and as it comes there are only three things you can do. One is not to go out, sell the car, and settle down with a good book, like this one. Another is to develop what many Americans have learned to possess, a gift for diminished literacy, a faculty for never seeing and hearing. And the third, of course, is to lie back, enjoy it, and havernize day.

2. GOVERNMENT BY WANTING

As we have seen, it is the great discovery of the consumer society that everything can be made better by words, and that, whatever it is, it has something to recommend it. You may remember the days when the word 'desire' had an awful lot to do with sex; well, it still does, but it also refers to that strange, salivating emotion we get when we see some-thing new in the shops or hear of something new on the market. It is an emotion that is stimulated everywhere, but the problems of shaping and channelling it are considerable. Happily we have in our society an ever-increasing number of persons skilled in doing just this – the traffickers in desire, the subtle seducers, the want-creators, who function much as do the bureaucrats of a communist economy, matching, with extraordinary skills, production to consumption, desire to necessity. How is wanting turned into needing? The modern world has found a wealth of ways. Consider just a few of them. You can, it has been found, make people want something by:

(a) offering them something else with it – a teething ring, say, for twenty soap flakes box tops. Chances are that if people don't want one thing they will want the other, and end up with both.

(b) telling them that their social status and the world itself will change once they have it in the house.

(c) hinting to them that it is inadvisable to be thrifty, and that they might as well spend all they have, and more.

(d) telling them that everyone else has *(i)* got it, *(ii)* intends to have it, *(iii)* would have it but unfortunately they can't afford it. The assumption of this kind of economy is that everyone wants what everyone else is having; it is true that there is a minority of persons who only want things – like Victorian furniture – because everyone else is getting rid of them. *This is a perversion*; and it soon rights itself, since as soon as people really want such things there grow up factories to make them.

(e) telling people that it is so new that no one has ever been able to want it before.

(f) telling them that persons they regard as their heroes – be they top people or top-of-the-bill people – have it.

(g) making it clear that if they don't get it now, they will miss the chance completely and for ever, for the fashion will be gone.

(h) making them realize how terrible are the things that they already have.

Finally, of course, you can make them want something that they didn't want before either by putting the price up, or by telling them that they can have two of it for the price of one.

But all these are, of course, traditional selling arts, and the reader may be looking for the modern difference. The difference lies in the atmosphere in which all this goes on; it lies in short in:

3. GOVERNMENT BY CHOICE

In the traditional society, the most important kind of choices that people had to make were moral choices, choices between different courses of action, choices between good and bad. The kind of choices you made determined what sort of person you were, and where you ended up. Nowadays the most important choice of your life, according to the advertising people, is the car you choose, the toothpaste you buy, the house you pick. Like moral choices, they determine the company you keep. They don't exactly get you into heaven or hell, but into the earthly equivalent; for you don't simply buy a product – you become a member of a group. I nearly gave up smoking in America, though cigarettes are splendidly cheap there, because I didn't want to be pinned down. After all, traumas spring up – is it better to be rugged and virile (Marlboro), earnest and informed, a thinking man (Viceroy) or smart, exclusive and fond of toy soldiers (Benson and Hedges)? At one point I developed a tremendous guilt about not smoking Viceroy, a brand I didn't like, because on the television commercials they used to have scholars who, after inhaling with one of those vast, unreal advertisement puffs that take the smoke down into the bladder and then regurgitate it, would say with classic simplicity: 'I smoke Viceroy – they have the thinking man's filter, the smoking man's taste.' It wasn't until someone explained to me that the hidden point of the advertisement was to provide reassurance about lung cancer – to say, in short, that you wouldn't die – by indicating that intellectuals had judged the odds and decided to go on smoking, that the guilt started to go away.

The consumer society goes in for choices.* Indeed, it insists that you choose; there are more brands of anything than you actually need. In present-day America you spend all your time choosing between things that you don't want to choose between; American Ford can theoretically run at full production for a year without producing two identical cars. What you are *really* choosing between is not goods but labels – the goods within are, actually, more or less the same. So, then, the consumer society insists that you choose – but when you choose it makes no difference, because you still get the same thing. In fact choice is in many ways actually prevented, since the essential differences between products are ironed out, so as not to confuse you *too* much, and marginal differences substituted. And the reason you get the choice is to fulfil *you*; goods don't just add a little to your life, they provide you with your identity. You can buy intelligence with a packet of cigarettes, charm with a bottle of lotion, and girls with a tube of deodorant.

In the consumer society people are given the choice between good and bad, so that they can pick whichever they like best. In this, however, they do not go unaided. There is Fashion to help them.

* As the television advertisements say (quoting, actually, George Eliot, who as scriptwriter only gets small print): 'The strongest principle of growth lies in human choice.' The question to ask, I always feel, is what is the choice between? The television advertisement goes on to say: 'The choice, for example, between joining the seventeen million people who, every Sunday night, turn for entertainment to the London Palladium; and being present with the panel of *Free Speech* at a discussion of current affairs.' This, like many of the consumer society's choices, is in fact a nonchoice, and my own impulse is then to move into another field of choice altogether – to choose, for example, to read the works of George Eliot, who sounds much more interesting.

In traditional societies people throw things away because they are worn, and purchase things because they need them. There are changes of taste, changes of fashion, but the change comes over a long period of time and is expressive of new and developing forms and fresh social thinking. In the past Fashion was, by and large, the spread of educated ideas, circulating through the society over the course of half a century, and being ousted when, after much time had passed, something better came along. Fashions were usually introduced by top people and spread downwards, servants being dressed in the last fashion but two. Moreover, fashion was weighed against morals, and use, and necessity, and only certain things were affected by it.

In the consumer society, everything is. In such a society no one knows his place, knows how or according to what rules to act and whether what he has got is what he deserves or whether, really, he merits something better. He does not know what is best or right – but he does know what is fashionable. In the consumer society fashion does not mean improvement, advance and development but simply *change*. The logic of fashion has become economic instead of educative; and thus the idea of taste has altered too. Taste means, not being able to pick the better from the worse, but being in on what is going. Moreover in the traditional society fashions were made by lords, sages and experts, while in the consumer society they are made by the press, by advertisement, by the popular song. Further, they are not personal but mass – within a fortnight the whole consuming public can be refashioned, save for those few who have whimsical, unchanging tastes and who look simply out of place, out of date and out of luck.

Fashions now enable people to live in groups. It was once possible for people to have the attitudes of a beatnik and yet not dress like one, or know that beatnik was what one was. Today this would lead to all sorts of complications, since one would be unidentifiable – and in fact beatnik is now not an *attitude* but an *appearance* (just as not all teddyboys were hooligans, but simply wanted people to think that they were). In this way, you tell the world who you are by being identified with a set *whose manners are already known*; and if the class system is disappearing the group-system is coming in. The point is, actually, to be In – but In, of course, with the people who are In. What is In with people who are Out is, naturally, automatically Out to those who are In. And in fact those who are Far Out, really Far Out, are often most In, since their group is hippest, most arcane. (The words Hip and Square, of course, are the words of a new class system; they provide a means of excluding people who don't think as you do. Likewise the word 'dig' means that one is temperamentally open to the fashion-information of the smart underground.) However, in these days of press publicity, and of creeping sociology – where if you do something new it is described by sociologists so that others can do it – what is In among Out people quickly is taken up by the people who are In, so that Out people have to drop it and find something else which is Out. Thus in America it was the people who were Far Out who took up, as a gesture of rebellion, the foreign car, cars so small that getting into them was a womb-like experience. This was a satisfactory gesture of protest against four headlamps and tailfins until it was taken up by suburban executives, the Men Who Have Everything, and made In. Now every square has one, except the people who are Far Out; they have sold theirs and gone in for old Cadillacs and motor scooters. Thus fashions start among protest groups, who are dedicated to taking dope and overthrowing the government, and end up in Levit-town.

Further, fashion now works by an ever-increasing shortening of the cycle of time which things are in. What is normal (i.e. what is fashionable) nowadays changes so rapidly that only the most avaricious reader or newsgetter can keep up. The cycle of change is now so short that there is rapid obsolescence of everything from last year's cars to last year's ideas. This is called the Ten-Minute Revolution, and means that the mind is usually empty and the dustbin always full. (In a consumer society, the focal point of the house is the dustbin.) The Ten-Minute Revolution already operates in America, where everything you buy has some device in it to show in what year it was made. And since, as I have said, a man these days is placed and identified by the goods he buys – indeed, this is his means of identifying himself – it has to be not only of the right year but also of the right brand and in the right conjunction to all other possessions.

The point here is that if you know who you are and what your status is, and if you live in one place among people who have known you since you were a boy, you don't need fashion. It is only in an anonymous, mobile, ever-changing society in which your identity seems to alter from day to day that fashions run your life, and that people look at their car and their kitchen to remind themselves what kind of people they are and what their social role is. 'I am I,' said Gertrude Stein, 'because my little dog knows me.' But I am I, says man in the consumer society, because I am fashion-conscious, spending-prone and have brand preferences.

5. GOVERNMENT BY PUBLIC RELATIONS

Public relations does not refer to the number of the Prime Minister's relatives who are in government, nor to the fact that in order to appear on television one no longer need have talent but simply be related to someone who has. Public relations are those relations with members of the public (persons are no longer, in this world of ours, persons; they are members of the public, labour units, and the like – they are defined by the rôles they have and not by who they are) on which the consumer society depends. When someone complains that something seems to him corrupt, inefficient, ill-conceived, badly-made or simply evil, a public relations man is a man who can give good reasons why it is all for the best.

Traditional societies have no need of public relations; they prefer, instead, private relations. There was a time when people were to blame for things; now the blame lies with departments and corporations. I can remember the days when you could go into shops and be served by people. In those days of autonomous choice, people often liked goods that shops didn't have; and if you explained this, the people in the shop would order it. Moreover you could ask them what they thought of their stock; they would tell you this was not so good, that better. This was called Personal Influence and was very reliable. Nowadays if you go into a shop and ask which product is best, they will read you the label on the packet (assuming that you are illiterate) or sing you the television commercial (taking it for granted that you are). Most have no idea what the goods they sell are like; moreover not only do they not know whether a product is good – they don't know what the word good *means*. They will tell you that it is 'cheap' or 'new' or 'popular'. Will tell you, that is, if you can find anybody in the shop at all. Nowadays, all the assistants are hidden behind mirrors in supermarkets, looking out for kleptomaniacs; for since supermarkets rely on impulse buying, they have to cope with impulse stealing.* Further, these shops don't belong to anyone; they are run by an IBM machine in London.

Public relations is to consumption what time-and-motion study is to production. Indeed, public relations men are the mediators of our society, and their influence is exerted not only forward on consumption but back on production. They advise producers when to smile and then they trot

* The anonymous society inevitably produces different attitudes toward crime. Before small private shops had been driven out by the supermarkets with lower overheads and bulk-buying, they encouraged honesty; one didn't want to steal off old Harry. But it is different when one is cheating the Inland Revenue or stealing from an IBM machine; one isn't stealing from anyone at all.

back to the public and tell them when to return the smile. There is the famous case of the American hospital which developed a machine which could deal with two diseases – one common and one rare. Public relations men advised it to save the machine for the rare disease – because it was more newsworthy. Public relations is the modern equivalent of what used to be called goodwill – except that the goodwill becomes, simply, a technique. It used to be thought that if you made a better mousetrap the world would beat a path to your door; but in the consumer society the fact that the mousetrap was better would be of small importance unless your public relations is good. The motto of the consumer society is that good wine *does* need a bush, and if it has a good bush it doesn't matter whether the wine itself is good or not.

Public relations start from the assumption that whatever is is right. The reason people dislike anti-semitism is, it hasn't been put over properly. Or take spiders – the trouble with spiders is, they project a bad image. A good public relations man, hired by a Spider Promotion Council, could soon put spiders back on the map. He would point out that spiders are industrious creatures, good husbands and fathers; the reason that they have all those legs, which people don't like, is that they have to spend much of their time walking on thin strands of web, a highly skilled occupation; spiders eat flies only when hungry, and because flies spread diseases; spiders have played part in history; spiders are by appointment to the Scottish Royal Family. Public relations likewise explains why changes cannot be made; currently, for example, the Electricity Board is spending vast sums in advertising to explain why they have to spoil the landscape by putting up overhead transmission wires and pylons, instead of – as in the traditional society – spending this money on research to find cheaper ways of putting the cables underground.

In non-consumer societies people live by personal relations and Word of Mouth; only in a vast anonymous society do we need public relations at all. In fact, public relations are taking over the equipment of private relations – human decency and respect and politeness and civilization still have their place in the consumer society, because, you see, they sell things. Dr Ernest Dichter tells us in his book *The Strategy of Desire* that motivation research has taught him that, when undertakers go to a house of mourning, they should ask not 'Where's the body?' but 'Where's Mr Smith?' Thus courtesies that were once performed because human decency demanded them are still done, even in the mass society – they are good for business. That old, close friendliness between man and man has not gone, though it may be used differently; if you fail to renew your subscription to *Reader's Digest* you will receive a letter from a most amiable, modern-sounding girl saying that she is your friend and that she will be miserable until you renew. In this sense, the consumer society is a pleasant and lulling experience, like stepping into a warm bath, and goodwill will remain in style as long as public relations finds it useful.

6. GOVERNMENT BY HAPPINESS

At one time it was only the Americans who believed in happiness. Rather, what they believed in was the pursuit of it; 'Life, liberty and the pursuit of happiness' were America's unalienable rights, rights the English always regarded with suspicion. The British with invincible good sense preferred being moral to being happy, and understood that many things that bring happiness are not moral. Moreover, happiness is a bonus and not a right; you can't legislate for it. Thus work was moral, while the devil found work for idle hands to do. The Americans, who used goods to increase leisure, we called materialistic. It is noticeable that this complaint has faded in recent years; and the reason is not that America no longer is, but that we now are.

We are, in short, being sapped at by creeping happiness. Growingly we expect above all to be delighted, entertained and amused at whatever cost. Dr Dichter has told us that puritanism, with its stuffy attitudes towards work, thrift and morality, is out of date – except for Samoans, who need to work harder still, in order to catch up. Modern society requires a new, lightweight morality. This is Instant Happiness. Drip-dry, no-crease, easy to take, Instant Happiness comes in all sizes and to suit all pockets. For that feeling better feeling, that feeling better taste! At all shops! Ask for it by name!

Instant Happiness is entertaining, light and easy to do, involving no energy and no work. Consider, for instance, the recent change in the meaning of the word *educational*. Once it meant 'enriching, elevating, enlarging'; it now means 'of little or no entertainment value; fuddy-duddy; square'. One of our current problems is to divorce our school and university system from the smear of being educational;* the Minister of Education has recently pointed out that some forms of education are congenitally dreary, and if they can't smarten themselves up they had better go. Universities, once communities of scholars, are now popularized as teenage paradises, full of dating, marching and hooliganism of the better sort. Or take another word, *cultural*, which now means 'the interests of a

* In America, after the sputnik, it was realized that education was useful after all, and here's how it was rehabilitated. Pat Boone, a teenage idol, ran an article in a magazine saying 'It's smart to be smart. The very latest thing I've learned in Teen Time slogans is one I brought back with me recently from a Southern swing. Down yonder the high-school set is saying, "It's smart to be smart!" . . . You don't have to be from Parentsville these days to get the news, and every teenager knows right well what's going on in space, not to mention what's doing on our own personal planet, Earth. . . . That's why it's of tremendous importance for you to meet the challenge as a crowd by *making learnin' loveable* . . . when the *crowd* decrees that It's Smart to Be Smart, you and I know it's the most effective method to release a new atomic power on the waiting world – the power of all your young minds and high IQ's functioning in high gear.'

small vociferous minority group, whose taste must be indulged occasionally because they still have some access to the means of communication'.* Or consider, finally, a third word, *paternalistic,* one of the dirtiest words of our time. In traditional societies 'taking a fatherly interest in, trying to guide from the point of view of superior wisdom, taste and authority' is considered desirable. The consumer society has, however, abolished fathers; the path of aspiration and order is now quite out of style, since it runs against our modern hedonism. The BBC used to be paternalistic, which meant that there were lots of good programmes on and when you opened the *Radio Times* you could find out what they were. Now the BBC has lowered the standard of programmes, the disc-jockeys assume that the world is as stupid as they are, and now, in the new, unpaternalistic *Radio Times* it is impossible to find out without a trained guide what is on the radio at all.

In this way, by abolishing difficulty and banishing authority, the consumer society seeks to make the path to happiness much more direct. However, the consumer society cannot actually give you happiness; it can only give you an indication of the means to it, which is of course purchasing, having things. When the Americans spoke of their right to the pursuit of happiness, the English used to smile in a superior way to themselves, knowing that if you actually *have* happiness you don't need to pursue it. It is only the discontented who must do that. So what, in fact, the consumer society does, to help you on your way to happiness, is to provide you with the promise of happiness – and the discontent to set you on your way towards it.

* Hence the effort that the Revlon Corporation of America makes on behalf of culture in its television shows. *The New Yorker* quoted an executive as saying: 'We've had a lot of culture on that show, David. A lot of things the intelligentsia would want. Sir John Gielgud, standing in front of a fireplace, with well-dressed, beautiful people around, reciting Shakespeare.'

PART EIGHT

MONEY – WILL IT SURVIVE?

This is a book about change, and how to live with it. But, you may protest, the changes that have been dealt with are essentially superficial, touching the surface of life, but leaving what lies beneath it intact. This is a natural enough English response; alas, as with so much else, it does not succeed in facing the fundamental nature of what is happening. In order to bring that home, it is, unfortunately, necessary to speak a little about the one thing that, in decent society in Britain, is and should never be mentioned; as with all taboos, the silence means that we are in the presence of the most important thing of all. The matter I am referring to is, I am afraid, money; and we may be sure that if, in this world, money is changing, then everything else is.

Think of money as it was. Think, if you will, of banks. There was a time, in this country, when a bank really looked like a bank. Solid, sturdy and aggressive, grand, exotic and expensive, banks spoke in architecture of the Victorian attitude to money – an attitude, of course, of acute veneration for the man who knew how to use it. The ethic by which he operated was that of self-help; and it was, indeed, of helping oneself that one always thought when one saw the stained glass, the cathedral pillars, the solemn inward gloom of the old British bank. As an American friend of mine once remarked, with surprise, after watching a whole row of Ealing comedies on late-night television: the most typical English sport was never hunting after all, but robbing banks. And doubtless this was true, once: every decent English gentleman surely nurtured somewhere in his bosom the dream of getting away with it, making the perfect haul, emptying the coffers in a way so perfect that no one would even know it had happened. Like any temple or place of power, the bank, as it was, represented a challenge. It was filled with money detached from any real ownership, already drifting back toward the government that had made it in the first place; it surrounded the stuff with dignity and protection, a sacred aura that naturally challenged the decent sporting instincts. When you went in, you could actually see the stuff, and observe all the rituals of veneration that went into making it all seem real. People carried money about; others sat at tables, counting it, popping it into sacks, weighing it. Going into the place to deplete one's account, it was almost impossible not to consider ways of augmenting it.

I am getting old now, and I am talking, of course, about the good old days. For my attitudes, in responding thus, were surely those of any reasonable old-fashioned Puritan. I believed, really believed, in religion and the rise of capitalism, and was delighted to see the two being put together. A sense of solemn worship affected me; I really felt that the bank manager was the true social arbiter of the community, its real priest, because he touched money more often than anyone else. And so naturally, when I entered the august establishment, built in Victorian Gothic and larger than Westminster Abbey, and I watched the busy, solemn bank-clerks, fine-looking men who devoutly studied the *Financial Times* every morning, understood its hermetic signals, and therefore knew what was *really* going on in the world, I dreamed dreams, like the one I had about robbing the place through the sewers and drainpipes, with a complicated system of pulleys. The point is that it was not entirely wrong, any more than it was entirely wrong for Alec Guinness to pull off the job in the old films. I was in a place of worship, and I wanted to share in the presence.

But this was indeed in the good old days, and, of course, the style of our banks, the look and feel of our money, has changed completely, so that it is hardly worth having any more. Remember the old English money, and how remarkably august it all was. The English banknote was a work of art, a finely scrolled document so prettily done that one's desire was to possess it, not to part with it in exchange for something totally inferior. But the banknotes that have come since, the banknotes of the new society, are quite different; smaller, flashier, they are, in effect, no more than the paper they are made of, reminding us that money is not reality but illusion. It seems amazing that anyone should change goods for them, though of course the goods themselves have lost in solidity, become compact, plasticated, miniaturized. Now possession of a banknote confers neither good feeling nor status on a man; it is an inferior form of credit card.

And the change has now penetrated from the money to the bank itself. The bank-temple has become an anachronism; a new kind of institution, more like a bingo-hall or the lounge of a pub, lightweight, frivolous, insipid and effete, trades in and stores one's worldly wealth, the sum of the labour of one's hands or one's mind. No longer is the atmosphere one of worship; as in some church of a new and modern faith, one is no longer being awed by money but invited to feel casual and offhand in its presence. There are banks designed to make you feel as though you are on an ocean liner, or in a coffee bar, or at a rather louche party. Banks listen to you, like you, pleasure you; even the bank manager is someone to like rather than be frightened of, a terrible shift in any good man's sense of the true order of things. Similarly something has happened to the bank-clerks. Once they were sober young men, conscious that they had in their keeping the true life-blood of society. Now they are mostly women, deeply unfiscal, spendthrift-looking souls who appear likely to go off on a shopping spree at any moment. I have only to look at them to feel at once insecure, remembering, as I do, that some of the money passing so lightly through their manicured and nail-varnished fingers belongs, after all, to me. I gather that this change in spirit stems from a discovery by, as you'd expect, the motivation-research people; the banks are stepping forward into the consumer society. Motivation research has discovered that many people are afraid of banks; if they want money, they prefer to go to someone who cheats them but makes them feel like a human being. In consequence, banks have decided to let up on the terror. One can't help feeling that this is, quite simply, a mistake. Surely the terror was quite proper, and made one realize how big a thing money is, and what an awesome world you confront when you deal in it. But of course this attitude, in the consumer society, has rapidly to be dispelled. The business of the old bank was to *keep* money and watch it very carefully indeed; the purpose of the new bank, however, is to get money out of there and into creative circulation. Spending must take place; it is not having money, but having spent money, that confers status. Hence the last thing the modern, up-to-date banker would want you to think of him was that he deals in *cash*. He deals in shares and bonds, and he finances things, but he doesn't touch money.

This is why banks have grown mild; and soon banks in England will look like banks in America, where they are made to look like a part of your own home. Some have all-glass fronts, so that they appear to be a part of the street. Others have their vaults open to view, so that there is no mystery about what happens to it when they've got it. There are patio banks, and drive-in banks where getting a loan is like buying a hamburger. There is a bank in New Jersey that has a women's banking room, with special desks and lounge chairs for children and a basket of free nickels for putting in parking meters – the nearest thing, up to *now*, that banks have got to giving away free samples. But that will come. There are already banks that give away floor lamps and toasters – whereas in the old banks you were given the feeling that you were privileged to be allowed in a bank at all; you were given, simply, *status*. Soon America will have travelling banks that come down your street ringing a bell, like the ice-cream man. Already the fun ethic has entered banking ('COME IN TODAY OR TOMORROW — THIS IS THE PLACE WHERE IT'S FUN TO BORROW' says a sign over a bank in Boston). The credit card, by which when you buy something you just sign for it, the layaway plan, by which you can die now and pay later, and banking by mail are now standard ways of dealing with money in America.

Perhaps, however, the real indictment of the American system is the fact that bank robbery no longer seems to attract the same class of person. The modern method in America is sly and seedy; it is to hand a note to the clerk, demanding that he or, more usually, she fill a paper bag full of bills immediately, and threatening to blow up the place with a concealed bomb, which, in most cases, the robber does not in fact have. The modern bank robber lacks panache and a sense of adventure; he usually turns out to be a timid man or an elderly lady who wouldn't frighten anyone except an impressionable young woman. I suspect that American banks are beginning to realize that things aren't what they were; they have started to put up notices that say 'Holdups in this bank are filmed', and, indeed, this may well do a lot to attract back to bank-robbing the right type of person. Next to putting up advertisements saying, 'Try the First National for your next holdup', I don't see that there's much more that can be done to bring back the good old spirit of free enterprise and self-help.

Nonetheless, all the evidence to hand would suggest that English banking is going the way of the American. One would have never thought that the time would come when banks were out to please you – what a strange reversal of precedence *that* sounds! Yet already there are advertisements designed to suggest that the English bank is letting up on the grandeur – that its premises are not, after all, marble and gold, but are like any other shop you go into; that its managers are not ogres, but thoroughly pleasant, amiable fellows, capable of creasing into a smile at the first opportunity; that bankers are not like eunuchs, employed to protect the harem inside from what they themselves cannot have, but like librarians, better pleased when the goods are all in circulation than when they are all in stock. Money, we are being told, is fun.

Can money survive? Can it, that is, retain its old authority and its old lure? It seems that it cannot. Already there is talk of a new lightweight coinage to go with the new lightweight attitudes. Think of the English penny; savour its medallion-like quality; consider how painful it always is to spend it on a mere bus-ticket or a visit to the lavatory; compare it with the flimsiness of the American cent, which one is all too glad to drop down gutters in the road or spend on a chocolate mint at the cashier's desk. The penny is the coinage of thrift. But modern money, like modern houses, cannot be built to last; it must be made of the flimsiest materials and given to us in the most offhand spirit, in the hope that we shall consume or destroy it as soon as possible. Nor is lightweight money to be the end of it. There is a yet more horrifying threat, that of decimal coinage. Our present coinage, which is gothic, sophisticated, and intellectual, with its peaks and sub-peaks, rises and falls, is surely the invention of a society of the greatest subtlety and intelligence; you have to be clever, just to buy things. But decimal coinage is all straight lines, like modern architecture, dull, flat and demotic, and its effect is to make people simpler than they need be. And what decimal coinage really means, of course, is that money isn't absolute. It is something that can be altered and changed at will. At one time it was only the Cottons and Clores, the people who rubbed money together to make it grow, who saw that money was not a religion but a game. Now, if we have decimal coinage, we shall all learn it; and the real lesson of it all is that money is not what we are given to save but to spend, and that man is put on this modern earth to buy all he can and use up what he buys, in order that he can say, at the end of his lifetime, that he has spent more money to less use than anyone else, and so left the world a better place.

PART NINE

THE
PUBERTOIDS

The world of the phogey may, then, look secure; but what we can say, on the evidence amassed, is that its survival never looked more doubtful, which does not, of course, mean that it will not survive. But can it, as it was intended to do, continue for ever? Or, to put the matter another way, is the phogey really going to be able to reproduce himself? This question calls for research into a phenomenon that has never really interested phogeys, the phenomenon of the young, that most unreliable of groups in any society, always allured by the new, tempted by change, and, on occasion, even conscious of being wiser than their elders.

Not of course in traditional or phogey society. For in that way of the world, young was never a very pleasant thing to be. It was always assumed that juvenility was an early stage of life's journey, and that it was only when a chap was initiated into manhood or, if necessary, womanhood that he or she began to find life at all interesting. The lesson was clear; any sensible person had no desire to prolong childhood a moment longer than was necessary, since it was simply not a real level of existence, one at which anything worth calling life actually took place. Thus, in the traditional society, the older one was, the better. The wisest people were those who had managed to live the longest, because they had learned all the knacks and responses that were fitted to living in a society which did not change very much. Father always knew best, and grandfather best of all; grey hairs conferred dignity, won respect and reward; and so Authority *had* authority, and one of its tasks was naturally to repress, educate and control the feckless and expansive instincts of anyone younger than oneself. It was true that, in this traditional type of society, it was always extremely difficult to think of anything useful for young people do do at all. Their tastes, when left undiverted, were naturally for unbridled sexuality and fighting, and though on occasion this might prove useful more often it proved no more than a standing embarrassment. Matrimony and sports were invented to cope with the problem; but the crucial instruction always given was for young people to grow as old as they could as quickly as was possible. The infant prodigy and the rapid learner were the ideals of society; education was devoted to the production of small mannikins. Responsibility came early; all the values that a chap needed to live as a grown-up were supposed to be internalized by the age of about eleven. In short, the rôle of children was to be inferior adults, and the best way to deal with them was to conceal them in nurseries and boarding schools until they had grown enough to conduct themselves decently in adult company. People used to say that children should be seen and not heard, but, reasonably enough, they were not fond of either alternative. So children deferred to their elders, imitated them and strove to be like them, and there was no such thing as youth culture – since, if youth had a culture, it could only be inferior, and therefore nobody would want to hear about it.

Thus the problem of the traditional society was to find something to do with the young before they become people. For this purpose the notion of Original Sin was invented. This – to put a theological crux quite simply – was the theory that people were evil until they were twenty-one; and it was never hard to amass evidence of this fact. Give the young money, and what did they do but spend it foolishly? Give them the freedom to order their own lives, and what did they do but indulge in folly and licence? Let them out of the house and what did they do but marry feckless beggars, or gamble, or consort with others of their own age in disreputable pursuits? It was clear that good sense demanded that they be locked up or heavily supervised until they were too old to enjoy having experience, and then, and only then, to let them have it. But of all the cogent rules devised in order to make this form of society work, there was one above all that was crucial. Whatever you did with your children, however nice you chose to be to them, to indulge them, to give them delights and fripperies, you should never, never, never let them keep the company of their peers.

*

And so it was until the consumer society came along, at which point every single one of the problems reversed. For, in consumer society, it is old that is not a very pleasant thing to be. It is senility that becomes an absurd late stage of life's journey, and it is when a chap is initiated into manhood or, more probably, womanhood that he or she begins to realize that life is dull. The lesson is therefore clear: any sensible person chooses to prolong childhood as long as is possible, for being older is not a real level of existence, one at which anything worth calling life takes place. In the consumer society, the younger one is, the better. The wisest people are those who were born yesterday, have the newest scram, the latest news, the most up-to-date info., for they have not yet become stuck with the knacks and responses so unfitted to living in a society which changes all the time. The young always know best, and one of their tasks is to repress, educate and control the instincts of anyone older than themselves. Likewise, the problem of consumer society is what to do with people after they mature. It is extremely difficult to think of anything useful for them to do at all. Their tastes, when left undiverted, are for sitting down in front of television sets with cups of Horlicks. *Come Dancing* and Scrabble were invented to cope with the problem; but the crucial instruction always given is for old people to get younger as quickly as possible. The jitterbugging granny and the senile delinquent become social ideals, and the role of adults is to be inferior children. Adults defer to their children, imitate them and strive to be like them, and there is no such thing as adult culture — just the noise of the pop-music coming up from the cellar, where the kids are.

The problem of consumer society is to find something to do with the old after they stop being people. Appropriately, therefore, the notion of Original Sin has been taken away from the young, and given to the old. It is they, after all, who are to blame for everything: for having made the mess we are all in, for being too repressive and paternalistic, too carping and critical, for having, in short, got out of date by living far too long. It is therefore they who sully and soil the intrinsic innocence and novelty of the next generation. Original Sin thus becomes the theory that people are evil once they are over thirty, and it is not hard to amass evidence of this fact. Give them money, and they spend it foolishly; let them out of the house, and they consort with others of their own age in feckless pursuits. Clearly good sense demands that they be locked up or heavily supervised until they learn to be young enough to enjoy modern life, and even then they will always be an embarrassment, since in the traditional society the young could always, without effort, get older, whereas the reverse is far more difficult. Thus, where in the traditional society everyone can't wait to age, and life begins at forty, in the consumer society no one can stay young enough long enough, and life begins to end at twenty. And where, in the traditional society, young people were thought of as imperfect adults, now adults are thought of as failed teenagers. Every society creates the heroes it needs: there was a time when the hero of the British was the Venerable Bede, and now it is Cliff Richard.

This change has been noticed in most modern societies; it certainly now exists in Britain. The old view, that innocence is a bore and lack of experience a handicap, is rapidly changing; now it is only those who are pristine who are wise and real. Hence it is part of modern life that most people spend most of it on the shelf. Medical advance has made puberty sooner and life-expectancy longer; this means that we will in fact spend much of our days looking with envy on the spectacle of a few young persons enjoying themselves in public until, by inexorable laws of modern wastage, they too become too old and must, at the age of twenty-one, retire. That envy no doubt always existed, but there was always a compensation; the older you were, the more money you had. But, in the new society, this is ceasing to be true. No longer are wages low when you are young, increasing when you have responsibility. Now it is the young people who have loose money to spend, and indeed this is what makes them such essential figures in the new consumer society. Hence the market itself is increasingly geared to products directed at and intended for the young: the clothes, the music, the technological items, the make-up, the buttons and badges, all point at the young, the ideal modern consumer, spending not necessarily wisely, but very well indeed. Thus consumer culture itself is a form of youth culture. In traditional societies, the young must make do with adult culture, and catch the crumbs off the table; so *Gulliver's Travels* was written as an adult satire but then adapted for the needs of children. In consumer culture, the reverse is true, which is why the most popular television programmes are those where adults are to be seen playing children's games. Involved in this is a ritual self-abasement now common among the older members of society; it is very important to learn how to appear less intelligent or responsible than one might actually be.

*

To put all this in another way: in consumer culture, there are no fathers any more. Traditionally what was good enough for dad was good enough for everyone else; now, of course, it is no good at all. Parents are no longer the model of what anyone wants to be; rather they are the model of what any young person in his right mind will try to avoid being. For in fact the most important thing about youth culture is that it is a culture on its own. Of course, it is consumer culture that celebrates youth for its own good commercial reasons; but youth also celebrates itself, forming, as it now can, a force, a peer-group, a self-contained domain that functions according to its own generational laws. It is not from the foreman or the teacher that people take their view of life, but from those of their own age. They connect, in fact, not with the past but with the present: which means, in a sense, that they connect with nothing, since that present is itself disconnected and has no founding substance other than its own mechanisms and commercial enterprises.

But if it is true that the young no longer have mothers and fathers in any but the most nominal sense, it is likewise true that the mothers and fathers have no children any more, except in the most nominal sense. Remember those amenable youths who fetched in the coal and lit the fire before going off to school to study hard to be great men and a credit to their parents; they are gone for good. For they belonged to the old days when families socialized the young, and therefore felt some responsibility for them. Now that the young are socialized by each other, and by the endless boom of communications which feeds them their music and their images of self, parents can only sit transfixed as incredible looming figures, the domestic house-yobs, rage through the premises, preening, cavorting and being as completely young as they can be. Under the clown-like costumes, the unbelievable hair-styles, the paint and the make-up, there may be the child one once nurtured, appearing in mysterious glimpses; but it is like an intergalactic visitation, a descent from another planet. And so it is; for these people who occasionally visit our houses and, in some sudden access of hunger, consume all the food in the house before departing, late at night, to the place they call 'out', are the Pubertoids.

*

It is, of course, consumer society that has invented one of the most original of modern concepts: that of the teenager. The species is new, and of course in traditional societies did not exist at all: in such societies there were, indeed, persons between twelve and twenty, who were not yet fully grown, and whose judgments were thought fallible and whose tastes seemed inclined toward immaturity, but for these people there was no name. They existed, but nobody knew that teenagers was what they were, all the time. Now that concept has been recognized, and indeed has spread to become a state of mind, to the point where it is now possible to meet middle-aged teenagers or even elderly teenagers, sitting on the beach at Malibu in topless bikinis. Teenager-ness is a condition, but of course it is above all one that is associated with the young, and is indeed now the mainstay of youthful existence. Thus it is quite probable that many teenagers would not have teenage problems if they didn't know that teenagers were what they were. For, of course, teenage and problems go together, and anyone who is a teenager and has none can only be an adult in disguise. In addition to problems, they have delinquency, which is quite different from other people's delinquency. In fact, in a consumer society, to be a teenage delinquent with prob-lems shows a conspicuous adjustment to the modern world.

This suggests that youth is actually a form of protest against the kind of society we live in, but this is not at all the case. In fact the protest is part of the style of the kind of society we live in, and the most pressing of fashions — fashion being, we recall, the essential motor or mechanism of consumer society. We hear much of the rebel without a cause; in fact to be without a cause these days is simply evidence of failure to shop around. For really there is no shortage of them ('Why are the drinking fountains in the park not working? Why do some cinemas close the ventilat-ing fans during the interval between films?' demands, urgently, one current cause, the campaign for Votes at 15). The teenager, kitted in leather, blue hair and flick-knives, may look like trouble, and actually *be* trouble. But that is not because he or she is the deviant in the new society, rather its maximum point of expression and consumption. And no doubt as time goes on we shall all grow more and more like them: having our problems, displaying our delinquencies, dancing to the drum of the peer-group. For, in the modern consumer society, how else, really, is there to live?

PART TEN

THE
POOR
MAN'S
GUIDE
TO THE
AFFLUENT
SOCIETY

A nd thus we come to the crucial question of this book.
How, indeed, between the world of phogey, and the
world of the Affluent Society, might one manage to live
some sort of ordinary, satisfying unaffluent and straightfor-
ward kind of life? The problem came to me when I was
living in America, and realized I would never make a
consumer; and then again back in England, when I realized I
would never make a phogey. We will explore a few of the
possible solutions in a moment, but let us just look a little
more deeply at the problem. For it will be quite apparent to
the intelligent reader of this book — like yourself — that if
contemporary society was completely unpleasant to live in,
nobody would do so. Equally it is clear that, if its diseases
and uneases had one simple remedy, there would be a
publicity-conscious, semi-fanatical, demonstration-loving
protest group, decorated with an icing of distinguished
names, to bring it about. So you will not be offered, in these
pages, some panacea, some large-scale political or economic
solution; rather, perhaps, that typical note of haunting
doubt that seems the note of the age.

I have remarked that, while in a traditional society a man
must be what he is, in consumer society a man can be what
he chooses. This is an existential dilemma, singularly un-
nerving, since there is no way of knowing which of the many
choices on offer is right. This was brought home to me, in a
mild way, when, after living for months in the United States
in the various possessions I had brought with me from
England to defeat the cost of living, I ran out of razor blades,
and had to make my way down to the corner drugstore to

buy some. The druggist, neat in his white nylon coat, looked out at me over the beach-balls and the corn-cob pipes with which, for some reason, his emporium was decorated: 'For a medium, light, or heavy beard?' he asked. I stared and said: 'I don't know.' He looked back at me in amazement, or even a kind of awe. 'Where have you been all these years?' he asked, 'What part of the woods are you from?'*

I thought about the matter, and finally I explained to him that I just didn't have the technological sophistication to know; I still have to this day the electric razor he went on to sell me. But then I realized that all my life was like that: I had been wandering around the United States in a whirl of consumer confusion. For in America all is the same: martinis come dry, extra dry, or dessicated, with a choice of domestic or foreign gin, an olive or a twist of lemon, and so on, so that by the time you succeed in ordering one you rather wish you had never bothered. This fine grading applies to all things, including refuse – there is trash, and there is garbage, and social obloquy falls on those who fail to understand. 'What are you, mac, a beatnik?' my garbage man, before he stopped visiting me altogether, used to ask as I stood there before the pails in my dressing gown, having got the rubbish all wrong again. 'I'm an Englishman,' I said. 'The discerning of difference of kinds and degree has always been the mark of the civilized intelligence,' he roared at me through the window of his truck as he backed up; and he never came back after that.

And it was brooding on these experiences that I realized that, quite simply, I didn't have it in me to make a consumer. Every era has its misfits, and clearly I was one of them. I noticed that, for example, when I had to decide whether I wanted a pack of king-size cigarettes, or a packet of ordinary or serf-size cigarettes, my mind had a tendency to shift to a new field of choice altogether – like whether to continue smoking or give up. For all the two-page spreads and the

* Actually I'm not from the woods at all.

thirty-second commercials, I remained the kind of person who, when asked what brand I wanted, replied 'Any will do.' It was not that my attitude was anarchistic, simply confused. It was just that, when I went out, as I now rarely do, to shop a little, and found fifty brands of soap when all I wanted was one, I felt that the choice of two or three would suit me perfectly well, and give me the nice democratic glow of feeling that I lived in a free and open society. The truth, it came to be apparent, was that the rôle of consumer requires a lifetime of practise and initiation, and that, moreover, unless these initiations had been gone through and assimilated, as in my case they had not, then it was really impossible to make an impression on anyone in America at all. For in this ultimate consumer world the man who does not know what drink he drinks, and why, who does not know what make of car he prefers, and why, who does not know whether he prefers blondes to redheads, or big behinds to little behinds, has – like a savage in an art-gallery – no being at all, no self-appointed identity, no selective mechanisms for giving shape to his life.

In this dilemma, admittedly, everyone was sympathetic, everyone tried to teach me the way of things. Perhaps the first American ceremonial I was invited to, just after my first arrival, was to be picked up by good friends and taken off to the Piggly Wiggly, a supermarket that was roughly the same size as Westminster Abbey, and a good deal more pretentious. From the moment we left the car under the rabbit sign in the carpark, so that we could find it again, and the great glass doors of the premises flew open before my feet without intervention of human agency, I knew I was undergoing a profound educational rite. Commerce went on apace in the vast hall; neighbours chatted together over their laden carts, while their young stole rolls of toilet paper from nearby displays and tried to eat them; all was, in a sense, normal. Over here a chef in a great hat was roasting chicken; there a cook in a check dress was icing cakes; by the doorway a person dressed as an elephant (one assumed it was a person, but it could have been a very clever elephant) was shaking hands with people and talking about collecting books of stamps. Concealed loudspeakers gave off the Bayreuth Festival Company, cavorting lightly with *The Ride of the Valkyries*; concealed detectives peered out from behind the two-way mirrors on the walls. The aisles of goodies stretched off into the distant haze. I realized I was supposed to buy something.

It was not easy. The shelf in front of me contained small tins labelled Roasted Caterpillar; adjacent to these were Tinned Baby Bees, Fried Grasshoppers, Chocolate Covered Ants, Alligator Soup and a number of other items culled from the insect and reptilian realms. There were mysterious bottles labelled 'Liquid Smoke'. With a five-dollar food order the supermarket was giving away, entirely free, one piece of a thirty-item set of kitchen tools, or so the microphones announced. Then suddenly I felt that *I* was at the centre of it all, felt the whole place focused on me, Bayreuth, detectives, elephants, and ants. I suddenly realized that I didn't have the stamina or motivation for it all; I turned tail, handed over twenty tins of chocolate covered ants, got my free spatula, and ran for the rabbit in the carpark. Mostly after that I shopped at corner groceries, all the time wondering, however, as with a woman one has loved and lost, just what the Piggly Wiggly was giving away now, and to whom. What was missing? Motivation and information: those basic consumer skills. I have been going to America ever since, and I have still not even begun to acquire them.

Not that I am the only one. Some years later, a married man now, my hair cut and the cuffs on my shirt mended for the first time in ten years, I carried my spouse off to America, rented a house, and pointed the way to the kitchen. An hour later she came out, a tear or two in her eyes: 'I don't know how to work it,' she said. And indeed there was everything, in the form of a gadget: a cooker that could pre-set itself, cook the meat while you were out, and, if necessary, go next door to borrow a cup of sugar as well; a blender that turned your tie into a drinkable liquid; an electric shoe-cleaner that ran on its own in the night. All the food was pre-packeted, and labelled 'Untouched by Human Hand', though clearly not by the hand of science; curious concessions were made to human intervention, so that the cake-mixes generously permitted you to add one egg to them, or the salad dressings invited the provision of vinegar. Nature, having been taken out, was being put back: the potatoes were being dyed red to give them a more natural colour, and in Baltimore an advertisement for a dairy claimed it to be 'the dairy with cows'.

*

It was here, then, that I realized that the new order of society was setting a pace that was beyond me, and that I would need to do something about it, not because the world I had entered was harsh and impossible to live in, but because it in some way was not harsh enough. Was it the phogey in me that made me doubt? And what, if one did not quite wish to live like that, were the alternatives? There were people who protested about all this, but they protested in groups, while I have never found groups of more than two, and they heterosexual, of any interest whatsoever. There was the Beat Generation, a new life-style (people no longer have lives, but life-styles) which protested against the world by not washing, not working, and wearing tattered clothing, things I had been doing for years without knowing that it was a protest at all. There are, however, certain solutions that can be offered, and for the benefit of those who find themselves anxious or somewhat out of tune with things I propose to sum matters up by discussing three of them. These three simple devices are, in order: Voluntary Poverty; Voluntary Provincialism; and Voluntary Agrarianism (or Living With One's Belly Close To The Soil). One, two, or all three of these may be of some help.

In a consumer society, the class system must use what tools come to hand, and it becomes a general aim to state one's rôle and demonstrate one's prestige by having many goods and displaying them. This is called Conspicuous Consumption, and what it means is, to put it shortly, that there is no point in having a television set unless you also have an aerial on the roof to show that you have it. It means, too, that if your neighbour does what is now smart and has a carpet in the toilet, he has somehow to get you in there in order for you to see it; this steps up his entertaining. There was a time when the only people one wanted to prove oneself to were those one knew well; and this kind of thing was never a problem. It was enough if nobody save the other two titled families in the district knew that the diamond in your tiara was the biggest ever found; you had played your cards with those who understood the game. But now one's peers are *everybody*, and one is expected to prove oneself to strangers.

It is possible, and probably wise, to contract out of this system before it is too late. The answer is in what I have called elsewhere the new Conspicuous Inconsumption, and clearly in such situations it takes on fresh urgency. Have your bathroom taken out and turned into a pigeon-loft, and stake your prestige on a Shakespeare First Folio you have bankrupted your family to buy. Explain to your friends that you have sold your car in order to buy a collection of butterflies. Cultivate an atmosphere of spareness, of austerity, about you – the air of bothering only about essentials. Wear shabby clothes, and dwell in an unlikely house. *Confuse people.* It may be hard at first, but it shows you are serious, after all.

Voluntary poverty of the sort I have described has in fact been institutionalized by certain professions, where commitment to old-fashioned sorts of value is thought sufficiently pleasant and rewarding to preclude the necessity of offering a substantial remuneration. The teaching and particularly the academic, profession is of this sort. Since the entrant is clearly a believer in *education, culture, discrimination* and other liberal values of decreasing social use, he is encouraged to think of himself as marginal to the society by a symbolic poverty enforced by his salary. At the same time, he feels himself to be monastic; he has, that is, given up worldly goods in his retreat from the world. He does his work because he enjoys it, while in the rest of society, it is taken for granted, other people do not work for pleasure but for money. *Their* pleasure lies in consuming. With voluntary poverty, then, goes voluntary failure, or the enjoyment of one's uselessness. One group which has taken up the style of poverty and failure (besides, of course, the academic profession) is, as mentioned, the Beat Generation. The ideal of the Beat Generation is to live wholly deviant lives, pursuing deviant arts such as jazz, dope-taking and reading. Both the academic profession and the Beat Generation share a great deal, in situation and in sympathies, with a third deviant group. These are the criminal classes, who are now widely recognized to be in protest against the kind of world in which we live. The intending failure is advised to make his choice, bearing in mind that criminals are under no compulsion to publish.

There is however one important note to add. To suppose that poverty requires less effort or money than wealth, or that failure is simpler than success, is to misunderstand the cardinal rule, which is: *In an affluent society, failure is much more difficult than wealth; and it costs just as much.*

This observation – acolytes call it, for some reason, Bradbury's Law – is so evidently true, so clearly right, that it might serve as the moral for life in our modern world. In traditional societies wealth is conspicuous, while no one stands out by his poverty, for that is run-of-the-mill. In the consumer society, poverty is conspicuous. It is thus only in consumer societies that persons can voluntarily *choose* it – the point being that if you want to be a failure this requires much more dedication and conscious effort than if you want to be successful. And, as I say, this kind of failure is a component of a technologically advanced and rich society; elsewhere it would simply not be noticed. Like voluntary agrarianism, which I deal with later, it is pleasant to live as a peasant, as long as one isn't.

Failure, then, is harder; it is also more expensive. The reason for this is quite simple – in our time the individual taste and the specialized or cultivated interest, being the whims of a marginal group, are catered for only on occasion. And a taste for the rare is always expensive. The time will come when the man who likes home-baked, whole-wheat, brown bread will have to spend most of his income on it, and it will become a craving with him, and also a mark of his status – as once a collection of fine bindings was. Thus already it is very expensive to like good plays, because it is no longer economic to keep local theatres open when they can with ease be replaced by income-producing office-blocks; and so the play-lover must go to London, an increasingly expensive business. One has to travel miles to see modern art or to find a bookshop where the bookseller knows something about the books he sells; good design of any sort is expensive – particularly as it usually has to be imported. Since these are the sort of thing our failure is likely to be interested in, and since failure in this context means by definition having essentials other than the essentials of the broad run of society, the failure these days has to have a considerable income and a sharp eye for a bargain. The failure spends just as much money as the successful man, but he has nothing – or, at least, no things – to show for it; just the quality of his own self.

There is, then, room at the bottom. But there is one further disadvantage; and that is that fashion has a way of catching up with you. One has always to keep one step ahead, because once one gets into the fashion-cycle one is finished; and this is yet another reason why poverty is costly. The Beat Generation affords another example of this point; here competition now prevails as to who can find the dirtiest sweater, the tightest jeans. Moreover, competition transfers itself to other areas; and instead of the currency of competition being, say, washing-machines it becomes, say, women. I recollect the disastrous case of a friend of mine, a Professional Failure, who bought a television set and, thinking to exclude himself from the competitive system, put it in his bathroom. He is now on the point of selling the thing, at a painful loss, because he has discovered that several of his smart set friends now have television in every room of the house, including the one he has chosen. The lesson is that if one is going in for failure one must go the whole hog. It is no use having anything that can be taken up by others; or chances are it will be. The trouble is that deviance itself is now thoroughly fashionable, and one is hard put to it to plough an individual furrow through the mire.

2. VOLUNTARY PROVINCIALISM

There was a time when everyone used to have to go to London in order to find out what was happening, for London was where it happened. Nowadays, of course, communications insist on telling us, whether we want to know or not, and London comes to you. Moreover, London is not what it was; someone was complaining just the other day that, on returning to London, he found it 'increasingly brutish'; while one of our leading poets was remarking that he had to go north every so often in order to escape from international nothingness. Personally I incline to the opinion that the English provinces are the only justification for the continued existence of England at all. Of course this view is brash, unfashionable, naïve and, in a word – provincial. This is its attraction. For the provinces grow more and more attractive all the time – because of what they aren't.

London, and the south generally, is no place for the man who wishes to escape the consumer ethic. The place has a softer, fancier air, all suede shoes and Babycham, in which dalliance grows and keeping up becomes more insistent. It is fancy, fast-talking and smart; it is dapper, gin-drinking and manipulative. People wear shirts with big bold stripes on them; women are somehow a different shape. There are too many estate agents, too many flower-shops, too many beauty parlours; and too many people walking about the streets not doing anything. The people who have work don't do it; and those who do work hard are doing non-work. It is a civilization of middle-men, people who rub money between their fingers and make it grow. The provinces provide money, intelligence, opinion; what London provides is services . . . chain stores, television programmes and governmental supervision. The raw material in literary, intellectual and all other spheres originates in the provinces, and is processed in London; when you have a good idea, you bring it to London and there you will find someone who can use it. Southerners wear fancy corsets and bikinis, or hair-oil and neckerchiefs and cavalry twill; and their ethic is the ethic of *mmm! delicious!* The only advice one can offer to the man who seeks to live outside the consumer society is to pack his bags and leave quietly, taking the first train to the north.

For the man who does seek to escape will find that the provinces are, more and more, the north. For the provinces – non-London – are receding all the time. There was a time when Nottingham, say, was outside it all; now all the bookshops have started to close down, the chain stores have ousted the local grocers, wage robberies are all the vogue, and creeping Londonization has taken place. Similarly, we have just been told that London is getting too big, and that employers will have to move their businesses out of London into the provinces; and that Kettering and Wellingborough should be expanded into a sizeable metropolis to take them. But of course this isn't moving London out to the provinces – it is making more of the provinces into London, which is the modern trend.

The contemporary escaper thus has a very hard time of it.

With the provinces retreating further and further, year by year, it is his hard task to retreat with them. A progress report on this year will hardly serve for next year, so fast is the penetration developing. At the moment, it seems fair to say, everything south of Manchester should be regarded as suburban London, with the possible exception of a few elusive enclaves in the far west, like Cornwall and parts of Wales. But, as the bends on the roads are removed and the television signal spreads, doom is on hand for even these places; it's all becoming Whicker's World. Who do you know who does not, finally, want to appear in shot on television, back there in the crowd behind the vox-poppings of the latest and most fashionable shop steward, waving away to mum? People talk of a revival of regionalism, and of Scottish and Welsh nationalism, and very nice too; but it is all fantasy. We are all part of each other, irretrievably linked together in one electronic and growing web, part of the universal exchange system of the washing-machine, the Mars Bar and the television news. Go to whatever distant, offshore, rocky island you like, and live as you mean to; you won't be there ten days before the supply boat lands, and out of it will get two camera men, three sound men, a girl with a clapperboard, and a director expert in *cinema vérité*, along with an interviewer in a scarf who will explain to you, as he holds out the microphone, that your relationship with the puffins has attracted the interest of the entire nation.

This is because, as we have said, consumer societies do not believe in privacy. There was – or so the phogeys say – a time in England when the freedom of each man to live his own life in his own way was taken for granted; you could do what you wished behind closed doors and, so long as you were not threatening the monarchy or the established church, what you did was found extremely eccentric and therefore quite reasonable. But, if the Englishman's home was once his castle, it is nowadays expected to be – like all castles – open to the public. In short, then, the taste for retreat, self-enclosure and privacy, for escape from the centre, goes against the prevailing ethic; it becomes extremely difficult, and therefore extremely expensive to indulge. Once there seemed to be space for everyone and everything, almost too much of it; now one has only to see what estate agents charge for a few square feet of it to realize that those days have gone. In these days of intellectual, political and economic oligopoly, the man who tries to flee the centre for the circumference will find few places to go to. For, wherever you find to Get Away From It All, you will find that It has already got there before you. Once abroad provided an answer; now, whenever and wherever you travel abroad, you travel by the horde – on a package arranged by Horde Tours. Discover, at last, that remote South Sea Island you always wanted to take your eight gramophone records to; you will find that the Island of the Month Club has chosen it as their cut-price special. Yes, provincialism is in all right – which is why every contemporary British novel these days is set on a canal bank near Wakefield. But the very fact that they are being written up is a signal of something; the provinces, believe you me, are nowt like what they were.

Which leaves us, finally, with:

3. VOLUNTARY AGRARIANISM

Except, of course, the same rules apply, yet further complicated by the fact that one also has to like the country. The primitive is not to everyone's taste, as Sigmund Freud once pointed out. But, even if it were, there are in England very few truly primitive corners of the community left, and the real country is very remote indeed. I am speaking, really, of the *real* country, the country beyond gentleman farmer land. England, as we all know, is full of villages – villages, however, where all the farm-labourers' dwellings have been converted and have brass carriage-lamps outside the door; villages where the rectory, redundant to ecclesiastical need, has been sold and is now lived in by a nationally-known poet famous for taking off his trousers at the Edinburgh Festival; villages where the green has been turned into a roundabout for the articulated lorries thundering through the night en route for the channel ports; villages where the duck on the duckpond has been tied down to stop it escaping back into nature. Nature, indeed, is a place no one can escape to. That classic haunt of solitude is solitary no more. The Lake District is now fuller than Oxford Street tube station, and people for whom a primrose by the river's brim a yellow primrose is to them come in their thousands, trampling down the primroses. At Thoreau's Walden Pond, near Concord, Massachusetts, you will find notices to trippers, announcing by-laws that firmly forbid all praying and meditation. The countryside everywhere is now filled with people hunting for privacy in very large groups indeed.

As for the old self-sufficient communities, well, these, as we have seen, have all gone by the board. Serfhood may be rewarding, but it is no longer possible. Farming is a way of running a factory in tree-lined surroundings, until you take down the trees. Back to nature is not back to nature at all, but a way of leading an old life in a new sports jacket. There is no means of evading the supermarket or the chain store; 30 m.p.h. signs have been put up on the Isle of Wight to bring the people there the benefit of civilization. Personally I have tried to make my separate peace in the rugged, rural East Riding of Yorkshire, a traditionally neglected area in which there still remain a few people who have not yet been vaccinated, and where the older car drivers still know what to do when attacked by flocks of geese. It still retains something: though most of the locals have theatrical agents and ten screen credits for appearing as extras in wellie-boot dramas of rural life, a few forelocks, meant for touching, are still to be found, and for the moment we still have gothic buses, with pointed roofs designed by Pugin and Ruskin, to pass through the ancient city walls of places like York and Beverley. People don't talk of London much, mainly because no trains go there – though occasionally a few coaches are sent out from Hull to Doncaster to see if they can get attached to any trains that happen to be coming down from Scotland. The weather is quite different from anywhere else, being imported from Spitzbergen; and there is a sound regional consciousness, probably derived from the conviction that we will be the first to go in the event of nuclear attack, constantly expected from the direction of Lancashire. But everyone knows that everything is at risk. Murmurs have been rife, for the last century or so, of a Humber Bridge that will cross that protective estuary and open us up to poaching from Lincolnshire; already the town of Beverley is being dismantled to let people from the south get through it more quickly on the way to look for the sea, a classically futile human quest.

So voluntary agrarianism, or what some people call living in the country, is likewise not an unambiguous solution – even if you can find any country around to live in. And, if you do, there is no guarantee that it will stay that way, which is why the dedicated countryman is, like the dedicated provincial, in a state of permanent retreat. Yet it is the very sight of someone else retreating that, in the modern world, constitutes a challenge if not an insult to everyone else. Thus, in the part of the world where I live and am foolish here even to mention, villages exist in permanent fear of being described somewhere as 'Yorkshire's prettiest village', or even being put on the ordinance survey map at all. For the world is full of folk poised to act on just such information. Within days, if not hours, they have packed the village main street and are to be heard calling loudly for ice creams and public toilets. Meanwhile others of the party are busy scavenging around to find the most beautifully cultivated rustic garden, in order to deposit in it rusty tin cans and burst mattresses, that necessary equipment without which no trip into the countryside is complete. The alert village watcher will immediately recognize the signs, and know the consequences. Within a week, the Electricity Board will be around with the chain-saws, the County

Council will be arriving with the curbstones and the concrete lamp-standards, and your friendly neighbourhood speculative builder will be along with his pile of bricks and his plans for two hundred bow-fronted semi-detached chalet-bungalows. It is already, again, time for the man seeking contemporary survival to pack his spare socks and his paperback copy of *The Waste Land* into his handwoven briefcase, and light out, a lonely modern hero, for the ever-diminishing and probably completely overcrowded woods.

*

It cannot be called perfect advice; there is no doubt that contemporary escape has its troubles, illusions and agonies. Still, in modern consumer society, fortunate is that man who has all his chattels to hand, who can manage on his own, who has, in a word, no wants, or Wants. At least he does not need to depend on anyone else – a very necessary thing in a consumer society where the things one cannot do for oneself are always on the increase, while the interest and attention devoted to those things by the people who can actually do them are always on the decrease. (After all, work done well is anti-social because it lasts far too long, and those who are busy consuming have little time to work as well.) No, at least, in poverty, in the provinces, in the country, one stands a chance of finding the old friendliness, the old community sense, the old tough-mindedness mother used to make; and, if not, one can always hang on to the bottled runner-beans till society grinds to a stop. Of course it will be protested, by the doctrinaire, that all this is living in the past, and sentimentalizing it – the classic phogey disease, in fact. The only appropriate answer is to observe that, while the choice is imperfect, it is better to live in the past than to live nowhere at all. Indeed, for present-day man, it is a choice of thoroughly modern significance, and much to be recommended as a very unphogey-ish and forward-looking action indeed. And if anyone points out to you that this is a contradiction, which is actually what it is — well, ask them what could be more contradictory than the land we now live in, England, our England?

ARENA

RATES OF EXCHANGE
Malcolm Bradbury

Dr Petworth is not, it had better be admitted, a person of any great interest at all. He is white and male, forty and married, bourgeois and British – all items to anyone's contemporary discredit. He is a man to whom life has been kind, and he has paid the price for it. He teaches; that is what he does. He is also a practised cultural traveller, a man who has had diarrhoea for the British Council in almost all parts of the civilized or part-civilized world. And that is why he is here now, in the summer of 1981, in the capital city of a small dark nation known in all the history books as the bloody battlefield of central eastern Europe, travelling culturally. And preparing, though he doesn't know it – to lose more than his luggage.

ARENA

'Mr Bradbury has an excellent ear for dialogue, a
sharp eye for types and a witty line of irony.'
Evening Standard

THE AFTER DINNER GAME
Three plays for television

Malcolm Bradbury

An evening with the faculty of a new university where
plottings and pretences are served up with the prawns
and pheasant; suburban angst and the search for truth
and meaning amid the temptations and distractions of
beautiful Birmingham; the rise and fall of a young
man of artistic leanings as he is initiated into the rites
and ways of advertising. Here are three comedies
written for television by the incomparable Malcolm
Bradbury, each of them tartly funny and devastatingly
incisive – and each of them embodying the very best of
Bradbury.

ARENA

ARENA

'Extremely witty . . . Bradbury writes brilliantly'
New York Times

THE HISTORY MAN
Malcolm Bradbury

Howard Kirk is the trendiest of radical tutors at a fashionable campus university. Timid Vice-Chancellors pale before his threats of disruption; reactionary colleagues are crushed beneath the weight of his merciless Marxist logic; women are irresistibly drawn by his progressive promiscuity.

A self-appointed revolutionary hero, Howard Kirk always comes out on top. And Malcolm Bradbury dissects him in this savagely funny novel that has been universally acclaimed as one of the masterpieces of the decade.

'A gold medal to Malcolm Bradbury for the funniest and best-written novel I have seen for a very long time.'   Auberon Waugh, *Evening Standard*

ARENA

'A wealth of comic inventions . . . utterly hilarious'
The Listener

STEPPING WESTWARD

Malcolm Bradbury

James Walker is a trapped man; a dispirited novelist living a drab life in a grey northern city. He's only in his early thirties yet he feels, tired, flabby, out-of-touch and fed up.

Walker's liberation is at hand. He is appointed Fellow of Creative Writing at an American University: and, once installed, finds that his image is now that of Resident Angry Young Man. Two affairs and several social gaffes later, he is beginning to suspect that there is more to the uninhibited campus lifestyle of the 'sixties than meets the eye.